A BOOK APART   W9-BOB-262

Dear Reader—

The revolution we've been preparing for is finally here. Responsive web design taught us to stop pretending that our content should be forced into static, print-like layouts. But visual design was only half the story. Now Karen McGrane shows us how to stop planning for where our content will "live" on a "web page," and create content that embraces today's multi-platform, multi-context digital world.

There's no better guide to creating future-friendly content and systems. For more than fifteen years Karen has helped create more usable digital products through the power of user experience design and content strategy. One of the first hires at Razorfish in 1995, Karen built the studio's user-centered design practice, becoming VP and National Lead for User Experience.

Today, as co-founder and Managing Partner at Bond Art + Science, she develops web strategies and interaction designs for publishers, financial services firms, and healthcare companies. Karen is also on the faculty of the MFA program in Interaction Design at the School of Visual Arts in New York, where she teaches Design Management, helping students learn how to run successful projects, teams, and businesses.

At web conferences worldwide, Karen is a fiery and articulate advocate of great user experience design and future-friendly content strategy. Expounded from stage, workshop, and lectern, her ideas have powerfully influenced designers and writers around the globe. Now her most important ideas of the past several years come together in a brief book for people who make websites. We are delighted to share it with you, our brilliant readers. You will absorb these ideas in a day or two, and use them creatively for at least the next decade.

Yours,

Jeffrey Zeldman
Publisher

Jason Santa Maria
Designer

Mandy Brown
Editor

Karen McGrane

CONTENT STRATEGY FOR MOBILE

Publisher: Jeffrey Zeldman
Designer: Jason Santa Maria
Editor: Mandy Brown
Copyeditor: Krista Stevens
Compositor: Rob Weychert

ISBN 978-1-937557-0-89

A Book Apart
New York, New York
http://abookapart.com

10 9 8 7 6 5 4 3 2 1

TABLE OF CONTENTS

FOREWORD

WHEN PEOPLE develop websites they talk about users. Users are weird creatures with strange intentions. They click everything, even where they are not supposed to. They rarely follow instructions. They are unpredictable. And yet we must love them. That is our job. Even when they are hard to love, even when they send us angry emails or tweet about how stupid we are.

When people talk about content they discuss readers. Readers are a known quantity. They start at the top of a page and go to the bottom, sentence by sentence. Sometimes they might skim, but often they're fully engaged. They pause and think things through. They might even read the same section twice.

The reader is, of course, easy to love. Because the reader is us.

"It is better to have 100 functions operate on one data structure," wrote computer scientist Alan J. Perlis, thirty years ago, "than ten functions on ten data structures." He meant: focus on your data, then code around it. Applications are there to serve the data, not the other way around.

It's a simple lesson but hard to follow. Mobile websites and custom apps have proliferated at a furious rate. They are costly and complex and have special data needs; ministering to those needs can take away from your ability to create great content. Worse, there are ever-more platforms. There's iOS and Android and Kindle Fires and the web; email and SMS and Facebook, Twitter, or Pinterest. Every platform tells you that it's the best, that it is worthy of your time and attention. But there's always another platform.

Let's put it another way: it is better to have 100 platforms operate on one content model than to have ten platforms on ten content models.

There's a huge lesson in this book: that users have been readers all along. The rise of mobile platforms just makes this fact plain. Reader-users read differently than their forebears—they read Twitter to find links to long articles that will interest them; they switch between phone calls and the Kindle app. And yes, they watch video, play games, and listen to music. But language still knits it all together, and words have more work to do than they ever did before.

"The reader's freedom," writes the essayist William Gass, "is a holy thing." As content strategists we are responsible for preserving that freedom. It's a significant responsibility. Trust in the content, in the words, images, and experiences. Let content lead—the rest will follow.

—**Paul Ford**

INTRODUCTION

THERE'S NO SUCH THING as content strategy for mobile.
Wait! Don't throw the book away yet!

There is such a thing as a content strategy that plans for
how you'll publish and maintain your content across all these
new and emerging platforms: smartphones and tablets, sure,
but also smart TVs, refrigerators, in-car audio systems—even
the desktop web. But "holistic enterprise content strategy" just
doesn't have the same ring to it, right? Mobile's the buzzword
on everyone's lips right now, so that's the label we've slapped
on this problem.

When we talk about content strategy for mobile, we're
not talking about publishing different content to be read on
smartphones. That wouldn't be much of a strategy—who can
afford to create content for only one platform? If content strategy means developing a plan for how you will create, deliver,
maintain, and govern your content, then content strategy for
mobile looks at the special challenges in getting your content
onto a variety of devices, screen sizes, and platforms—including mobile web, native apps for iOS, Android and Windows,
and, yup, even the desktop.

When we talk about content strategy for mobile, we're also
not talking about delivering content to serve the "mobile context." "Mobile" seemingly implies motion, mobility. We imagine a hurried businesswoman, dashing through the airport,
glancing at the screen out of the corner of one eye. But like
the "dial" tone, the "return" key, and "cut and paste," the word
"mobile" has expanded to mean something different from its
analogue in the physical world. Anyone who's ever pecked at
his mobile phone from the couch, too lazy to walk over to his
desktop computer just a few feet away, knows exactly what
we're talking about. Anyone who's ever waited for hours in
that same airport, passing the time transfixed by a tiny glow-
ing screen, knows the same thing. "Mobile" doesn't necessarily mean you're on the move.

If mobile doesn't imply a specific device or a specific context, then what does it mean? The only thing it really tells us is that the user isn't seated at a computer, with all that tells us about the interaction model. With a desktop machine, we can assume the user has a monitor, and we can know with almost total certainty that the monitor has a resolution of 1024×768 pixels or higher. We can assume the user has a pointer, controlled by an external pointing device like a mouse or a trackpad. We can probably assume that the user has a broadband connection.

When we say someone is on mobile, all we know is they're using a device that is...not a desktop. We know very little about what they see and how they interact. They might have a tiny 240×320 BlackBerry Bold screen, or a glorious iPad 2048×1536 Retina display, large enough to rival even a desktop monitor. Their pointing device might be as direct as touching the screen with their fat, greasy fingers, or as abstract as navigating with a four-way rocker. They might have a connection that's no better than a 56K modem, or a connection that's as zippy as a full-fledged workstation with a dedicated T3 connection. All we know is that we can't really count on anything.

Daunting, right? How are we supposed to make good design decisions if we don't know the boundaries of what the user will see? How do we structure information, if we don't know how the user will navigate and make selections? Most important, how do we know what content someone's going to want, when we don't know anything about their context?

It seems that many businesses are choosing to answer these questions by hiding their heads in the sand. "No one will ever want to do that on mobile," they insist. "Only a fraction of our visits today come from mobile devices," they sigh. "Users need only location-based services on mobile," they say, stubbornly.

If there's one thing we should have learned from the web, it's that user behavior evolves more quickly than businesses realize. User expectations evolve and move forward, and only later do organizations hurry to catch up. If you're wondering if you're going to need to invest in getting your content on mobile, quit hoping you won't have to. Your customers are already there.

What you'll get from this book

This book discusses *why* and *how* to get your content onto many different devices, platforms, screen sizes, and resolutions. *Content* includes your text, images, videos, charts, and any other forms of information your reader might want from you.

While the smartphone isn't the sole focus of this book, many of the examples will focus on smartphones because they are both the most common device and most challenging form factor. Getting content onto mobile phones is top of mind for many organizations.

If you're stuck on whether and why to be on mobile, this book can help you make the case. You'll get data and statistics about how people use their phones today, including insight into emerging audiences like the "mobile-mostly" user. You'll also get analysis and rationale about why it's important to get *all* your content onto mobile—not just a subset that you decided was appropriate for the "mobile context."

If you want to know how to get your content (especially desktop web content) ready for multi-channel publishing (especially onto mobile devices) this book will help you get there. You'll learn about *adaptive content* and how this approach to structured content will help you publish flexibly to multiple channels. By creating presentation-independent content that includes meaningful metadata, you'll set yourself up for a future where your content can go anywhere.

You'll learn how to evaluate whether your current desktop content will work on mobile—and how to edit it down to provide a better reading experience for both desktop and mobile users. A content inventory and content audit will help you evaluate whether you should revise, delete, or keep your content as-is. You'll also figure out if you need to create new content by conducting a gap analysis.

Want to know how to structure your content so users can easily read and navigate it on a mobile device? You've come to the right place. While navigation models and screen layouts might differ for mobile, you can develop an underlying information architecture that will give you the flexibility you need.

You'll also learn how your internal processes need to change—your editorial workflow, content management tools, and organizational structure—to support great content on mobile. Managing people and process gets more complex when you're dealing with multi-channel publishing, and this book will help you make sure you can maintain your content over time.

What you won't get from this book

There are many topics, even some closely related to the themes discussed in this book, that I simply can't cover in one slender volume. Fortunately these topics have been discussed at length by other people:

- This book is geared toward organizations with dozens, hundreds, thousands, even millions of pages of content on a desktop website, most likely published out of a content management system, that now need to be published to new devices and platforms. If you build transactional applications—like web apps that enable people to manage their finances or personal health, or social applications focused on user-generated content—this book is not going to discuss how to adapt your application interface and interaction design for mobile.
- This book will not tell you whether you should develop a mobile website or a native application. There are good reasons for each approach, and others have covered this debate at length. This book will help you get your content into shape so that you can publish it to the mobile web, native apps, and anywhere and everywhere else you might want it to go. As a result, I'll often discuss mobile web and

mobile apps interchangeably. I know they're not the same from a development and interaction perspective, but from a content perspective, your goal should be to make it possible to publish to any or all of them.

- This book will not recommend whether you should use responsive web design or develop separate templates to cover different form factors. Again, there are lots of reasons, pro and con, for choosing one approach over another, and the decision depends on your unique situation. Because your content management infrastructure does influence which approach you choose, I'll touch briefly on this topic in this book. However, no preference should be taken for one approach over the other. Only you can decide what works for your content and your organization.

- I'm also not going to tell you which content management system is the "best" one. There are many, many factors that go into a decision of that magnitude. There's no best CMS, only the CMS that's best for you. If you're considering implementing a new CMS to help you manage multi-channel publishing more easily, I will offer some general guidance about what to consider—but I won't recommend a particular platform.

Let's kick this off by looking at *why* you need to get your content on mobile.

1 YOUR CONTENT, NOW MOBILE

WHEN WE TALK about how to create products and services for mobile, the conversation tends to focus on design and development challenges. How does our design aesthetic change when we're dealing with a smaller (or higher-resolution) screen? How do we employ (and teach) new gestural interactions that take advantage of touchscreen capabilities? How (and who) will write the code for all these different platforms—and how will we maintain all of them?

Great questions, every one. But focusing just on the design and development questions leaves out one important subject: how are we going to get our content to render appropriately on mobile devices?

The good news is that the answer to this question will help you, regardless of operating system, device capabilities, or screen resolution. If you take the time to figure out the right way to get your content out there, you'll have the freedom (and the flexibility) to get it everywhere. You can go back to thinking about the right design and development approaches for each platform, because you'll already have a reusable base of content to work from.

The bad news is that this isn't a superficial problem. Solving it isn't something you can do in isolation, by sandboxing off a subset of your content in a stripped-down mobile website or app. The solution requires you to look closely at your content management system, your editorial workflow, even your organizational structure. You may need different tools, different processes, different ways of communicating.

Don't despair. There's even *better* news at the end of this rainbow. By taking the time now to examine your content and structure it for maximum flexibility and reuse, you'll be (better) prepared the next time a new gadget rolls around. You'll have cleared out all the dead wood, by pruning outdated, badly written, and irrelevant content, which means all your users will have a better experience. You'll have revised and updated your processes and tools for managing and maintaining content, which means all the content you create in every channel—print, desktop, mobile, TV, social—will be more closely governed.

Sounds great, right? Well, to get there, you first need to admit you have a problem.

DO WE REALLY NEED TO GET OUR CONTENT ON MOBILE?

Do you have a website? Then you need to get your content onto mobile devices. Period.

Advertisers

Let's say your company advertises on television. Or maybe outdoors. Ads are expensive! Maybe you put a URL at the end of the TV spot, maybe you don't. Maybe you put a QR code on your billboard, maybe you don't. (Please don't.) Either way, if you're not considering what happens when your potential customer picks up her phone after seeing your advertisement, you're wasting money.

FIG 1.1: Apparently none of Pepsi's $1.7 billion marketing budget was spent on content for their mobile website.

Eighty-six percent of smartphone owners say they use their phone while watching television, and forty-one percent say they do it *every day.* The numbers are even higher for tablet owners (http://bkaprt.com/csm/1). Think all those dual-screen users are just tapping away on Facebook? Think again: seventy-one percent of smartphone users say they've searched for more information on their mobile device after seeing an advertisement on TV, in print, or online (http://bkaprt.com/csm/2).

What do you think will happen after someone sees your TV spot? She'll remember to look you up tomorrow, when she's back at her desk? She'll be satisfied to squint at your desktop website through her tiny little viewport? She'll really enjoy the error message that says Flash is required to view your website (FIG 1.1)?

Or do you want her to find engaging information about your products and services that will help her decide or make her feel more positive about your brand? A lot of rhetoric about "marketing to the mobile context" can be summed up simply: don't waste money on advertising if you don't have a mobile website to back it up.

Retailers

Retailers need to support three distinct mobile contexts.

First, they need to support customers who use their smartphones to "pre-shop" stores, compare prices, and look up product features and customer reviews before deciding to transact. Sixty-six percent of smartphone owners say they use their phones in just this way to become smarter shoppers (http://bkaprt.com/csm/3).

Second, retailers also need to support a truly mobile use case. During the 2011 holiday season, one-third of all American adult cell phone users say they used their mobile phone to look up information while physically in a traditional retail store—either product reviews or pricing information. How many sales are retailers gaining or losing because of information customers find on their phone—potentially information from a competitor? It's clear that mobile phones influence purchase behavior: when people used their phones to look up pricing information while in-store, thirty-seven percent decided not to buy the product at all and nineteen percent left the store and went online to buy the product (http://bkaprt.com/csm/4).

Finally, retailers need to support ecommerce shoppers who choose to transact on their phone instead of on the desktop or in-store. Those shoppers have high expectations: eighty-five percent expect the mobile experience to be equal to or better than the desktop web, and eighty percent expect the experience to be at least as good, if not better, than shopping in the store. Unfortunately, the real world doesn't live up to their expectations: eighty-four percent of people who have transacted on mobile report experiencing a problem, including error messages, wonky navigation, or insufficient, incorrect, or confusing information (http://bkaprt.com/csm/5).

Part of the problem is that only thirty-seven percent of retailers have a website that's compatible with mobile browsers, and only twenty-six percent of those mobile websites rendered properly in all six major mobile browsers. Apps don't offer much salvation either—only twenty-six percent of

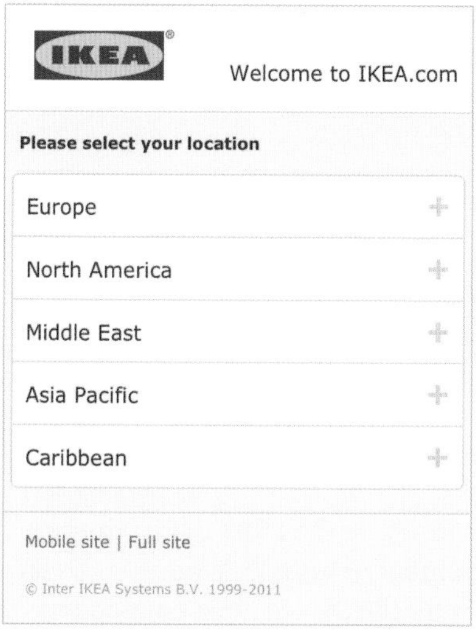

IKEA Welcome to IKEA.com

Please select your location

Europe   +

North America   +

Middle East   +

Asia Pacific   +

Caribbean   +

Mobile site | Full site

© Inter IKEA Systems B.V. 1999-2011

FIG 1.2: If what you want is a mobile-optimized country selector that will just dump you on the desktop site, IKEA has that in stock.

retailers offer any flavor of downloadable app (http://bkaprt.com/csm/6).

Shoppers deserve better than the superficial, unhelpful mobile sites even major retailers provide. Mobile sites that don't provide information, don't enable transactions, and don't influence purchase decisions really aren't very strategic (**FIG 1.2**).

Publishers

I have a print subscription to *The New Yorker,* which I read exclusively on airplanes during the twenty minutes around takeoff and landing, when electronic devices are prohibited. Recently, I was flipping through the magazine and came across a long article I looked forward to reading. "I've already saved this to Instapaper," I thought. "I'll save it until I can read it on my phone later."

Rich Ziade, CEO of read-it-later app Readability, shared insights from their analytics data in an email that show many people seem to enjoy—not just tolerate—reading on their phones:

People read on their phones...a lot. A device doesn't need to be the size of a book for people to want to engage it. In fact, the iPad is proving less than ideal for reading. The screens on our phones have moved beyond the BlackBerry. They're bigger and sharper and fit in your pocket. We read on our phone. Who knew?

Readability's data shows that users are even *more* engaged in reading on their mobile devices than on the desktop—and, surprisingly, on the iPad. In March and April 2012, the average time readers spent on the mobilized article view was even longer than the time people spent reading on both the desktop and on tablets.

Publishers, therefore, have one of the most demanding challenges in getting their content onto mobile devices. Users insist on consuming content on the device most convenient for them. A content strategy that limits access to a particular channel or device will simply alienate readers and send them to a competitor. Given the economics of the publishing industry, publishers need a content strategy that supports efficient and cost-effective multi-channel publishing most of all.

Financial services

More than any other industry, mobile websites for financial services seem to focus on supporting quick tasks for the on-the-go user. Many mobile websites for banks and investment firms offer transactional access only for current customers. And, of course, an ATM finder (FIG 1.3).

But users want more than just transactional capabilities and location-based services. They want information. Fifteen percent of searches for finance and insurance content come from mobile devices (http://bkaprt.com/csm/7; PDF). They're not all looking for the closest ATM.

Desktop websites for financial services firms, on the other hand, offer a mix of informational content and task-focused functionality. Visiting the desktop website, users can find product marketing, information about professional services, financial research and data, and tools to help make financial

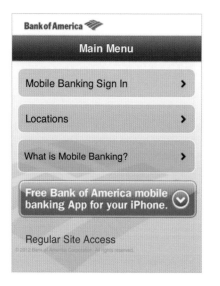

FIG 1.3: Bank of America prioritizes transactional functionality aimed at current customers, perhaps because it assumes you won't want to become a new customer.

decisions—all of this in addition to the transactional functionality available to customers behind a login.

Even if most users who visit a website for their bank or investment firm go directly to the login, that's not a reason to ignore all the other reasons that users might visit. Information about the firm's products and services is just as important— optimizing for the main use case doesn't mean ignoring everything else.

Healthcare

Health organizations especially seek to deliver content via mobile devices. Personal, private, and always with us, mobile phones seem perfectly suited to deliver intimate information about our health and well-being.

It should come as no surprise that health information was the top-growing content category on mobile in 2011, with 18.5 million American mobile users accessing health-related content and information, an increase of 134 percent over the previous year (http://bkaprt.com/csm/8).

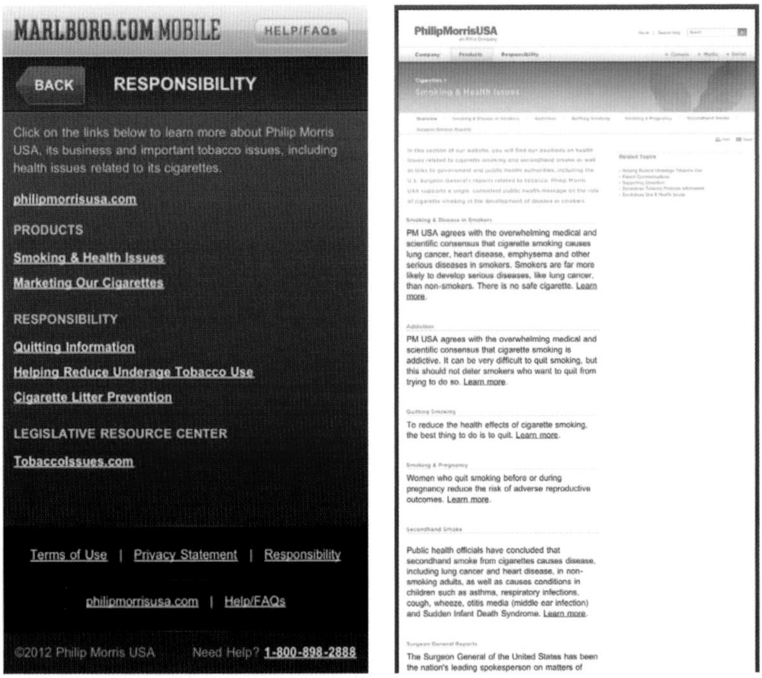

FIG 1.4: Tsk, tsk, Marlboro, making users pinch and zoom through a desktop site to find resources for quitting smoking.

Mobile phones are also a useful healthcare tool because they're so ubiquitous across age groups, income levels, and ethnic groups. They're especially powerful at reaching underserved populations, according to Pew Research (http://bkaprt.com/csm/9):

> If your organization's information is not available on a small screen, it's not available at all to people who rely on their mobile phones for access. That's likely to be young people, people with lower household incomes, and recent immigrants—arguably important target audiences for public health messages.

Whether you have a public mission aimed at improving health and wellness, or are a private company that needs to communicate with your audience about their medical and healthcare choices, getting content onto mobile devices isn't something you can ignore. You have a responsibility to make that content available on mobile devices. For example, Marlboro (FIG 1.4) is legally obligated to provide information about the health consequences of cigarettes and smoking cessation resources. But by forcing users to go to the desktop site to find it, they imply those messages just aren't as important as the marketing information available on their mobile-optimized website.

Universities

Universities have rightly invested in building mobile websites and apps for their students. Of course they have—you wouldn't believe how attached young adults are to their phones! (And even if you're not a university—if you're trying to reach teens and young adults, you'd better think about how to reach them on their mobile device.)

As of February 2012, sixty-two percent of Americans aged eighteen to twenty-four own a smartphone. When this age group buys a new phone, they're disproportionately choosing to buy smartphones: eighty percent of those who bought a new phone in the previous three months chose to get a smartphone (http://bkaprt.com/csm/10). What's more, forty-two percent of smartphone owners aged eighteen to twenty-nine say they mostly go online using their phone—they rarely use the desktop web (http://bkaprt.com/csm/11).

Universities have invested in building mobile websites and apps aimed at current students. Campus maps, building phone numbers, and parking information are available in a mobile-optimized version at most universities.

Here's the problem: it's not just *current* students who might want information about the university on their phones. It's also prospective students. As of March 2012, thirty-one percent of teens aged fourteen to seventeen have a smartphone. That number is higher for older teens, aged sixteen to

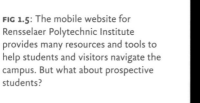

FIG 1.5: The mobile website for Rensselaer Polytechnic Institute provides many resources and tools to help students and visitors navigate the campus. But what about prospective students?

seventeen. Teens whose parents have a college education are also slightly more likely than other teens to have a smartphone.

As you might imagine, teenagers use their phones to go online. Over the course of a month, ninety-two percent of teen smartphone owners say they've used their phone to go online. Guess what that replaces? Yup, desktop computer use. Teen smartphone owners say they're less likely to have used a desktop computer than their peers who don't have a smartphone (http://bkaprt.com/csm/12).

While library hours, campus shuttle schedules, and dining hall menus are readily available, admissions and academics information is notably missing (**FIG 1.5**). What about all the prospective students who will never see the campus tour or application deadlines because they're glued to their phones?

Restaurants

"Mobile users want to see our menu, hours, and delivery number. Desktop users definitely want this 1MB png of someone smiling at a salad."

—MAT MARQUIS (http://bkaprt.com/csm/13)

FIG 1.6: Now you can have the experience of not being able to get in to Per Se right on your phone! One of the finest restaurants in the world has one of the worst mobile websites.

Restaurant websites are justifiably mocked for being terrible. Flash intros. Menus only available as PDFs. Navigation that dances around the screen, just out of reach. Auto-playing audio files. They're like a guided tour through web design worst practices. But what's teeth-gnashingly irritating on the desktop becomes positively impossible on mobile (**FIG 1.6**).

Farhad Manjoo of *Slate,* in a hard-hitting exposé, tried to uncover the reasons why restaurateurs design websites that are an assault on good taste and seemingly hostile to user intentions. Along the way, he learned that mobile may just be the catalyst hungry diners need to prompt restaurants to design better websites: "I spoke to a few restaurateurs who've created great, easy to use, elegant sites, and they all said they were motivated by one thing: they were missing out on traffic from mobile devices," (http://bkaprt.com/csm/14). Small wonder: about thirty percent of searches for restaurants come from mobile, more than for any other industry (http://bkaprt.com/csm/7).

MOBILE IS NOT THE "LITE" VERSION

"It looks like you're on a train. Would you like me to show you the insultingly simplified mobile site?"
—CENNYDD BOWLES (http://bkaprt.com/csm/15)

If people want to do something on the internet, they will want to do it using their mobile device. Period.

The boundaries between "desktop tasks" and "mobile tasks" are fluid, driven as much by the device's convenience as they are by the ease of the task. Have you ever tried to quickly look up a bit of information from your tablet, simply because you're too lazy to walk over to your computer? Typed in a lengthy email on your BlackBerry while sitting at your desk, temporarily forgetting your keyboard exists? Discovered that the process to book a ticket from your mobile was *easier* than using the desktop (looking at you, Amtrak!) because all the extra clutter was stripped away?

Have you noticed that the device you choose for a given activity does not necessarily imply your context of use?

People use every device in every location, in every context. They use mobile handsets in restaurants and on the sofa. They use tablets with a focused determination in meetings and in a lazy Sunday morning haze in bed. They use laptops with fat pipes of employer-provided connectivity and with a thin trickle of data siphoned through expensive hotel Wi-Fi. They use desktop workstations on the beach—okay, they really only use traditional desktop machines at desks. You've got me on that one.

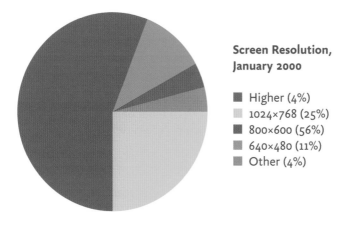

Screen Resolution, January 2000

■ Higher (4%)
▨ 1024×768 (25%)
■ 800×600 (56%)
■ 640×480 (11%)
▦ Other (4%)

FIG 1.7: We have plenty of experience delivering content to a variety of screen resolutions. Why do we assume that mobile screens necessarily indicate a different context?

Knowing the type of device the user is holding doesn't tell you anything about the user's intent. Knowing someone's location doesn't tell you anything about her goals. You can't make assumptions about what the user wants to do simply because she has a smaller screen. In fact, all you really know is: she has a smaller screen.

The immobile context

Users have always accessed our content from a variety of screen sizes and resolutions. Data reported by SecureCube shows that in January 2000, the majority of users visited from a browser with an 800×600 resolution, but a significant minority (twenty-nine percent) accessed the site at 1024×768 or higher, with a smaller percentage (eleven percent) viewing the site at 640×480 (http://bkaprt.com/csm/16; **FIG 1.7**). At that time, decisions about how best to present content were seen as design challenges, and developers sought to provide a good reading experience for users at all resolutions, discussing appropriate ways to adjust column widths and screen layouts as content reflowed from smaller to larger screens.

What you didn't hear designers talking about was the "640×480 context" and how it differed from the "1024×768 context." No one tried to intuit which tasks would be more important to users browsing at 800×600, so less important options could be hidden from them. No one assumed that people's mindset, tasks, and goals would be different, simply because they had a different-sized monitor.

Why do we assume that mobile is any different?

THE MOBILE-ONLY USER

"Mobile was the final front in the access revolution. It has erased the digital divide. A mobile device is the internet for many people."
—SUSANNAH FOX, Pew Research Center (http://bkaprt.com/csm/9)

The statistics about how mobile computing has changed human behavior often emphasize the developing world. Seventy-five percent of the population of India—approaching a billion people—has a mobile phone (http://bkaprt.com/csm/17). China now has more mobile internet users than there are people in the United States (http://bkaprt.com/csm/18). Of the ten million people in Egypt who access the mobile web, seventy percent of them are mobile only—they never use the desktop internet (http://bkaprt.com/csm/19). For billions of people in the developing world, mobile phones are the only way they will ever connect to the internet.

For many of us, those numbers seem positive and exciting, but remote. We might not be trying to connect with customers outside our own country, and we perhaps aren't looking to reach people in the developing world. We may never have a need to communicate with our audience using SMS, because everyone we want to reach has access to the web, email, and chat. We assume that a "mobile-only" user is as foreign to us as a villager in Africa, in India, in China.

We're wrong.

In developed nations, a large and growing minority of users are mobile only. As of June 2012, thirty-one percent of

Americans who access the internet from a mobile device say that's the way they always or mostly go online—they rarely or never use a desktop or laptop computer (http://bkaprt.com/csm/20). Those numbers are growing: the Pew Research Center reported in an earlier study from July 2011 that twenty-eight percent of smartphone users go online mostly using their phone (http://bkaprt.com/csm/11). While some of those users may also have access to a computer at home or at work, one-third of those "mobile mostly" users have no access to a broadband connection at home (http://bkaprt.com/csm/21).

And for those who would argue that mobile mostly users *can* still access your website via desktop, let's be clear about who gets to make that choice: *they* decide how and when they want to access your content, not you.

As of April 2012, thirty-five percent of Americans currently have no internet access at home. Sixty percent of Americans who make less than $30,000 per year don't have a broadband connection at home. About half of African American and Hispanic households don't have broadband access to the internet at home. And eighty-eight percent of Americans without a high school diploma don't have a broadband internet connection (http://bkaprt.com/csm/22).

But as of early 2012, eighty-eight percent of American adults *do* have a mobile phone (http://bkaprt.com/csm/23). As of July 2012, 54.9 percent of mobile users own a smartphone— and two-thirds of people who acquired a new phone in the previous three months chose to get a smartphone (http://bkaprt.com/csm/24).

As more and more people acquire smartphones, many people who don't currently have access to the internet will suddenly have it in the palm of their hands. A growing number of people who cannot afford to pay for both mobile phone and broadband internet access pick one device—the phone.

An April 2012 Pew Internet Project report on "Digital Differences" explains how mobile is changing the makeup of who has internet access (http://bkaprt.com/csm/22):

Groups that have traditionally been on the other side of the digital divide in basic internet access are using wireless connections to go online. Among smartphone owners, young adults, minorities, those with no college experience, and those with lower household income levels are more likely than other groups to say that their phone is their main source of internet access.

By 2015, more Americans will access the internet through mobile devices than through desktop computers, according to a prediction by International Data Corporation (http://bkaprt.com/csm/25). Some of these people may still have access to the desktop web, but for reasons of context, ease, or laziness, will choose their mobile first. For others, they will have no other way to view your content. For this growing population, if your content doesn't exist on the mobile screen, it doesn't exist at all.

The latest personal computing revolution

Before the personal computer put an IBM clone on every desk, computer usage was available only to mainframe users, who gained access to precious computing time via terminals, restricted to using the computer for only a few brief minutes or hours each week. Though personal computers lacked the processing power of a mainframe, what users gained in flexibility, speed, and the ability to directly interact with the machine made up for the deficiencies in the PC. People adopted this new computing technology and didn't look back.

For users with no home access to a desktop computer, it's not hard to imagine them as similar to the mainframe users of the past, signing up by the hour for a sliver of computer access at an internet café, a school computer lab, or a library. And like the PC before it, the smartphone will leapfrog these users past reserved-by-the-hour connectivity and onto an internet where they're in control. Will the limitations of the smartphone deter them, sending them back to the internet café when they have an important task? Not likely, or only in the most limited of circumstances. For an increasingly large segment of the population, the mobile computer will be their only computer. And like the mainframe users of yore, they won't mourn the desktop. Instead, they'll define an entirely new way to interact with the device.

No heads in the sand

"There is no reason for any individual to have a computer in his home."
—KEN OLSEN, CEO of Digital Equipment Corporation
(http://bkaprt.com/csm/26)

"There is no reason that anyone will need to do that on mobile."
—YOUR COMPANY, PROBABLY

Ken Olsen was the cofounder and CEO of Digital Equipment Corporation (DEC), the second-largest computer company in the US during the late 1980s, makers of the very successful PDP and VAX lines of minicomputers. DEC's downfall (the company was sold to Compaq in 1998) is partially blamed on Olsen's failure to respond quickly enough to the rising demand for personal computers. DEC struggled in the early 1990s to adapt its business away from its historically profitable line of minicomputers and toward a new line of microcomputers for personal use.

Right now, someone in your company is doing the same thing. Someone in your business is telling himself that mobile is a blip, a grace note, a mere satellite to the larger desktop website. A team of people are all agreeing that offering a full set of content on mobile is a "nice-to-have," something to think about only after investing in yet another redesign of the "real" website.

They're wrong.

Delivering content on mobile isn't an afterthought. It's a necessity. It isn't a luxury. It's a requirement. Do people want to look it up? They'll want to look it up on mobile. Do people need to search for it? They'll want to search for it on mobile.

Do people want to read it, deeply and fully? They'll expect to read it on mobile. Do they need to fill it out, document it, and enter it into the system? They'll need to do it on mobile. Think of any piece of information people may want to access on the internet. They will need to access it on a device that isn't a desktop website.

This goes double for any organization that needs to reach people outside mainstream desktop users. Are you a government institution? You have a civic responsibility to deliver your content to all your citizens, which means providing it to them on mobile. Are you an equal-opportunity employer? You're really not—unless you're delivering your content where African American and Hispanic users can find it. To reach all of these groups, you can't assume that they'll take the extra step to go find your desktop website. You need to bring it to where they are. Which is mobile.

MOBILE TASKS, MOBILE CONTENT

I recently departed Austin, Texas, traveling with three friends. Since we arrived at the airport a bit early, I wanted to lounge in the comfort of the United Club, away from the teeming masses. I felt it would be rude to abandon my friends to a similar fate outside, and so I wanted to know how many guests I could bring with me to the club.

A simple Google search should clear up this problem. Sure enough, I quickly found a link that seemed promising (FIG 1.8).

Alas, following the link to United Club Membership just took me to the homepage for mobile.united.com. When users search from a mobile device, United automatically redirects links from Google to its mobile website—without checking to see if the content is available on mobile. If the content doesn't exist on mobile, the user gets unceremoniously dumped on the homepage of the mobile website. Mobile redirects that break search—how is that ever a good user experience?

Sure, there's a link to the full desktop site, but that too just dumped me on the desktop homepage. I could try to use United's internal site search, but I'd wind up pinching

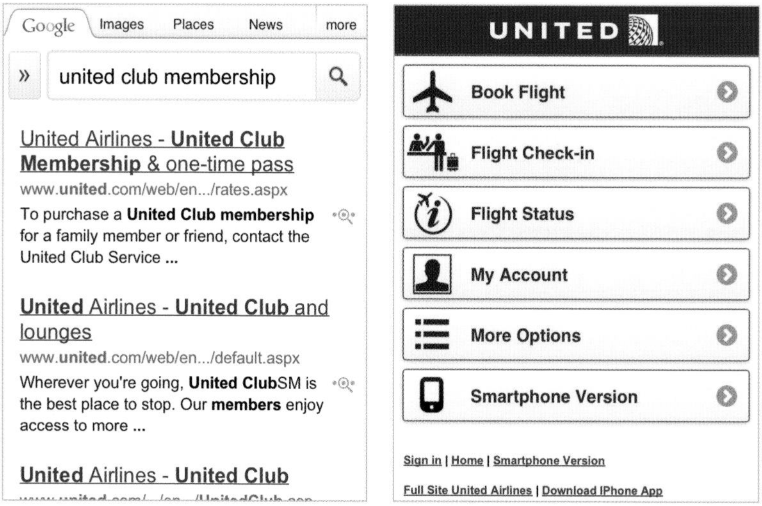

| Google | Images | Places | News | more |

» united club membership 🔍

United Airlines - **United Club Membership** & one-time pass
www.**united**.com/web/en.../rates.aspx
To purchase a **United Club membership**
for a family member or friend, contact the
United Club Service ...

United **Airlines** - **United Club** and lounges
www.**united**.com/web/en.../default.aspx
Wherever you're going, **United Club**SM is
the best place to stop. Our **members** enjoy
access to more ...

United **Airlines** - **United Club**

UNITED

✈ Book Flight ❯

Flight Check-in ❯

ⓘ Flight Status ❯

👤 My Account ❯

More Options ❯

📱 Smartphone Version ❯

Sign in | Home | Smartphone Version
Full Site United Airlines | Download IPhone App

FIG 1.8: Searching for "United Club Membership" shows that the content exists on the desktop site. But because the mobile website redirects the URL, users wind up on the homepage of the mobile site.

and zooming my way through several search result screens formatted for the desktop. And honestly: why should I have to? An answer that should take me one tap from the Google search results should not require searching and tapping through several pages on both the mobile and the desktop sites.

I went and asked the representative at the desk. (Correct answer: two guests.)

I don't bring this up just because I want to shame United for wantonly redirecting links to a mobile URL when the content isn't available on its mobile website. (That's a terrible thing to do, but it comes after a long list of other bad things I'd like to shame United Airlines for doing.) No, I use this example to illustrate a common misconception about mobile devices: that they should deliver only task-based functionality, rather than information-seeking content.

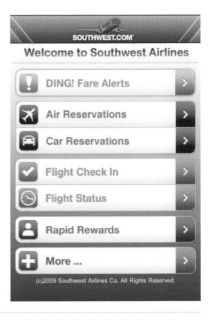

FIG 1.9: The Southwest Airlines iPhone application only has room for what actually matters...if what matters doesn't involve looking up information.

Information seeking is a task

Luke Wroblewski, in his book *Mobile First,* tells us that Southwest Airlines is doing the right thing by focusing only on travel tasks (**FIG 1.9**):

> *The mobile experience...has a laser-like focus on what customers need and what Southwest does: book travel, check in, check flight status, check miles, and get alerts. No room for anything else. Only what matters most.*

Mobile experts and airline app designers don't get to decide what "actually matters." What matters is what matters to the user. And that's just as likely to be finding a piece of information as it is to be completing a task.

Eighty-six percent of smartphone owners have used their phone in the previous month to look up information—whether to solve a problem, settle an argument, get up-to-the minute information such as traffic or sports scores, or to decide whether to visit a business like a restaurant (http://bkaprt.com/csm/27). Don't believe me? Look at your own search history on your mobile device—you've probably tried to answer all sorts of questions by looking up information on your phone.

The Southwest Airlines desktop website includes information about their baggage policies, including policies for checked bags, carry-ons, and pets, as well as lost and found, delayed baggage, and a variety of other traveler information, such as what to do if you lose your ticket, need to rebook, or your flight is overbooked. It even includes information for parents looking to book travel for unaccompanied minors, and how Southwest accommodates disabled flyers and the elderly.

The mobile experience does not. Who are we to say that this content doesn't actually matter?

It's fine to optimize the mobile experience for the most common tasks. But that doesn't mean that you should exclude valuable content.

Mobile is social

Have you ever clicked on a link from Facebook or Twitter on your phone? How about a link someone sent you in an email?

Of course you have. Sharing content with our friends and colleagues is one of the bedrock ways we communicate these days. Users don't distinguish between accessing email, Facebook, Twitter, or other social services on the desktop or on mobile—they choose them fluidly, depending on which device they're closest to at the time. In fact, as of June 2012, nearly twenty percent of Facebook members use it exclusively on mobile (http://bkaprt.com/csm/28).

If your content isn't available on mobile—or provides a bad reading experience—you're missing out on one of the most compelling ways to get people to read it. Is your site littered with icons trying to get people to share your content? If your readers just get an error message when they tap on shared content, all the effort you put into encouraging social sharing is wasted (FIG 1.10).

FIG 1.10: "No mobile content found. Would you like to visit the desktop version of the site?" asks *The Guardian*. Can you guess the answer?

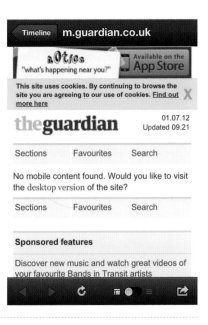

DESIGNING FOR CONTEXT

"Context" is the buzzword everyone throws around when talking about mobile. At the South by Southwest Interactive conference in 2011, the panel called "Designing for Context" was the number one must-see session, according to *.net magazine* (http://bkaprt.com/csm/29).

The dream is that you can tailor your content for the user's context—location, time of day, social environment, personal preferences. Based on what you know about the user, you can dynamically personalize the experience so it adapts to meet her needs.

Today, we use "designing for the mobile context" as an excuse to make mobile an inferior experience. Businesses want to invest the least possible time and effort into mobile until they can demonstrate return on investment. Designers believe they can guess what subset of information or functionality users want. Everyone argues that they're designing for the "mobile use case."

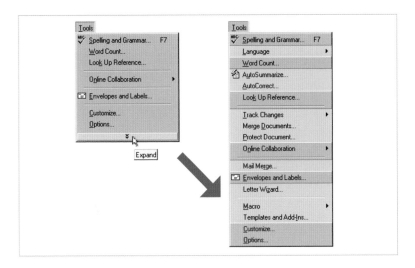

FIG 1.11: Personalized menus in Office 97 attempted to prioritize only the options Microsoft thought users wanted. They were a failure.

Beware of personalized interfaces

Presuming that the "designer knows best" when choosing how to deliver personalized content or functionality is risky. We're notoriously bad about predicting what someone will want. Even armed with real data, we're likely to make incorrect assumptions when we decide to show some things and hide others.

Microsoft Office tried this strategy in the late 1990s. Office 97 offered many new features and enhancements, which made the user interface more complex. Long menus and dense toolbars gave the impression that the interface was "bloated" (http://bkaprt.com/csm/30). Sound like any desktop websites you know?

In response, Microsoft developed "personalized menus" and "rafted toolbars" which showed the most popular items first (FIG 1.11). Although Microsoft had good data and a powerful algorithm to help determine which items should be presented first, it turned out that users didn't like being second-guessed. People found it more frustrating to go through a two-stage process, hunting through multiple menus to find what they were looking for. Personalized menus violated one of the core principles of usable design: put the user in control.

Now imagine that instead of clicking a chevron at the bottom of the menu to expand it, the user has to click a link to "full desktop website" and then hunt around in the navigation while squinting at a tiny screen. If your website's mobile version only offers a subset of your content, you're giving your users the same frustrating experience. Only much worse.

You don't have good data

Microsoft had a ton of data about which options people used most frequently. They developed a complex algorithm to present the default "short" menu based on the items people were most likely to want, based on years of history and research with multiple iterations of their product. And they still made mistakes.

The choices you make about which subset of content you want to deliver probably aren't backed up by good data. They might not be backed up by any research *at all,* just a gut feeling about which options you imagine will be most important to the mythical on-the-go user.

Even if you do have analytics data about which content people are looking for on mobile, it's not likely you're getting an accurate picture of what people *really* want. Today's crippled mobile experiences are inadequate testing grounds for evaluating what people wish they could do on mobile. As Jason Grigsby, Cofounder of CloudFour.com and MobilePortland.com, says: "We cannot predict future behavior from a current experience that sucks" (http://bkaprt.com/csm/31).

Context is the future!

Designing for context doesn't necessarily mean delivering less. In the future, it will mean prioritizing information differently, anticipating what the user wants based on known data about the environment or in response to the user's explicit request.

We're not there yet. To get there, we need to know a lot more about how people use their mobile devices. Contextual research, usability studies, analytics data, and participatory design are all tools that we can use to determine how best to design for context.

But none of that research will be meaningful if we don't have a full set of content to work from. If we want objective and accurate data about how people engage with mobile devices, we first need to get *all* of our content on mobile. Only then will we be able to get real facts and glean meaningful insights about what people want, when they want it, and how they want it presented. Until then, we're just guessing.

If your vision for mobile is designing for context, then the first step you need to take is getting all your content onto mobile devices.

ALL OF IT? REALLY?

Really. Your content strategy for mobile should not be to develop a satellite to your desktop site, showing only the subset of content you've decided a mobile user will need. That's not going to work because:

- People move fluidly between devices, often choosing a mobile device even when they have access to a desktop computer. Don't assume you can design for "the on-the-go user" because people use their mobile devices anywhere and everywhere.
- Mobile-only users want and need to look at your content too! Don't treat them like second-class citizens just because they never or rarely use the desktop. Even if you think of them as "mobile-mostly" users, remember that you don't get to decide which device they use to access your content. They do.
- Mobile supports reading content just as well as it supports functional tasks. Don't pat yourself on the back just be-

cause you've mobile-ized some key features—there's more work to do with your content.

- Context is a cop out. Don't use context as a rationale to withhold content unless you have real research and data about what users need in a given situation or environment. Unless you have that, you're going to guess wrong. (And even if you do have that—given the crappy experiences most users get on mobile today, you'll still probably guess wrong.)

You should aim for content parity between your desktop and your mobile experiences—maybe not exactly the same content presented exactly the same way, but essentially the same experience. Never force users to go to the desktop website for content they're seeking on a mobile device.

Freaking out? Convinced it's impossible to achieve content parity across all your devices? There is a way.

CONTENT BEFORE PLATFORM

ANY CONVERSATION about mobile seems to focus on these debates:

- Should we design a mobile website or a native app?
- Should we build separate apps for iOS and Android? What about building apps on other platforms, like Windows?
- Should we plan a responsively designed website that will adapt across desktop, tablet, and phones?
- Should we create a separate mobile website, with its own set of custom-designed templates?

From a design and development perspective, the answer to these questions is: *it depends.* There are good arguments in favor of each of these options. Speed, gestures, polish, discoverability, search, sharing, accessibility—all these and more come into play. There are plenty of pundits out there willing to argue with you late into the night about which approach is best.

But there's no point in debating the merits of the container if you don't know what you want to put in it. Or if you don't have a funnel.

The real problem for most companies isn't which format they choose to get their content on mobile. It's getting their content on mobile at all.

The answer to these questions—at least as far as your content is concerned—is: *yes.* Chances are, you will need to get your content onto the mobile web (responsive or no) and into native apps designed for iPhones, iPads, Android phones and tablets, Windows, and BlackBerry.

Like with the web before it, we've focused on talking about design and development before figuring out the content. We're so caught up in the excitement around gestures and geolocation, HTML5, and responsive design, that we've lost sight of mobile's real challenge. Which, like the web before it, is *content strategy:* figuring out how we're going to create, manage, and maintain our content across all these platforms and devices.

Our first-order problem is to develop processes and infrastructure to get your content into a format that your user can view on whichever platform they choose. What will your workflow be for managing content across platforms? Can you live up to the demands of regular multi-channel publishing, keeping everything in sync? Whether you want a mobile website, a native app, or both, designing and developing for that platform will be easier if you have a content strategy in place.

A SEPARATE MOBILE WEBSITE

Recently, usability pioneer Jakob Nielsen argued that you should "Build a separate mobile-optimized site (or mobile site) if you can afford it," where you cut features and content "that are not core to the mobile use case," (http://bkaprt.com/csm/32).

Mobile designers and developers responded swiftly to argue that creating a separate mobile website is a bad idea (http://bkaprt.com/csm/33). According to Josh Clark, author of *Tapworthy: Designing Great iPhone Apps,* suggesting that a separate mobile website is an appropriate strategy perpetuates "several stubborn mobile myths that have led too many to create 'lite' mobile experiences that patronize users, undermine business goals, and soak up design and tech resources" (http://bkaprt.com/csm/34).

Noz Urbina, Senior Consultant and Business Development Manager for Mekon Ltd., told me that the idea of a separate mobile website rests on a false expectation about how you will manage and maintain your content:

> The solution being a mobile site implies two falsehoods: that "mobile" is just one platform and needs only one site to solve it, and that maintaining separate sites per platform is going to be a sustainable strategy. Your content is a constantly evolving body of assets that must be maintained, and the same users will be accessing your content in various ways. Sites like Facebook, eBay, Amazon, Evernote, and myriad more are setting a market expectation that no matter the mode of interaction, content should be consistent, relevant, and up-to-date—regardless of how it's accessed.

From a content strategy perspective, the risk of developing a separate mobile website is that you'll wind up maintaining duplicate content in multiple places. News flash: this will be a disaster. Separate processes. Out-of-sync updates. Wasted effort.

The reason a separate mobile website is dangerous is that, in general, you want to avoid creating multiple versions of your website. It's called forking, and it's a forking nightmare from a maintenance perspective. If you fork your website into separate mobile and desktop versions, then you're stuck updating both every time there's a change. Avoiding this problem is tricky, even with sophisticated content management systems. But before we get there, let's start with a simple scenario.

Manage content like it's 1999

Imagine you have a static website that you created back in the late 90s. There's no CMS, so all the content is hard-coded into your HTML. (If you can't imagine any organization still living in these dark ages, take note that fifty-seven percent of domains under development by American federal agencies are not being built with a CMS: http://bkaprt.com/csm/35; PDF.)

You decide that you want to join the twenty-first century by creating a mobile website. Good for you! Except for the nightmare part, which is that you'll essentially create a totally separate website, and now you must update both versions every time there's a change. You must code two completely different sets of pages: unique templates for both desktop and mobile. And even if—especially if—you want to publish exactly the same content to both places, you must maintain two separate versions of the content too. Double your workload, double your fun?

Cut features! Cut content!

Great! You might think creating distinct content is actually an advantage. A separate mobile website will still be aces if you don't want to publish exactly the same information. Cut features, cut content, and re-prioritize your messages. You'll publish a mobile website that only shows a subset of content, targeted specifically at the mobile user's needs.

Let's set aside for a moment the argument about whether or not that's the right user experience. (It's not.)

From a maintenance perspective, you're still forking your content. Want to add a new page? Edit a description? Fix a typo? You'll be doing it twice.

But that's why I have a CMS

The whole point of having a content management system is to help streamline the publishing workflow, right? So of course, you just assume that your current CMS will make it easy to publish content to different channels and platforms.

Jakob Nielsen makes this assumption when asked about the dangers of forking your content (http://bkaprt.com/csm/36):

I would assume that most industrial-scale sites would be generated from a single back-end product database and content management system, with the different designs represented by templates and rules about what information goes into what version.

Unfortunately, today, many CMSs don't easily support this type of multi-channel publishing without considerable investment in custom development. Ask your CMS to display similar-but-not-the-same content in different templates according to a set of business rules, and it'll start spewing out yards of dot-matrix printer paper, beeping that it "does not compute." True multi-channel publishing isn't built into low-cost or even mid-range CMSs—usually only larger enterprise CMSs designed to support publishing to both print and web can handle it.

You have a Web CMS

Many CMSs are designed to publish to one and only one platform: the desktop web. In a Web CMS, content authoring and management functions are "coupled" with content publishing and display functions. (If you have a large-scale enterprise CMS, it's likely "decoupled" and this point may not apply to you.)

Most websites simply don't have a content management backend that will support populating different design templates with different content. Content assets (like text fields, images, and supporting media) are usually locked to a specific output format or design. That wasn't a problem until now, because no one expected the CMS to have to support publishing to different channels—the desktop web was all there was.

The fact that the CMS works this way is no mere implementation detail. Unfortunately, it's fundamental to the way content is published on the web today. We've got to fix this if we're going to deliver optimized experiences on desktop and mobile.

Multi-theme management

Now, some CMSs do, in fact, support publishing content to multiple templates. Publishing the same content to different "themes" allows a WordPress blog or a Drupal site to have separate templates for desktop and mobile content display. Note that says "separate templates"—not separate content. These CMSs still like to publish the same content on both sites. (Specifically, they're happy when publishing the same blob of "body" or "node" content one-to-one across desktop and mobile. Other content elements, like sidebars or user comments, are often stored in a different location and may be stripped out.)

What these CMSs don't do (at least not without putting significant effort into it) is support publishing different content to different templates according to a set of business rules. So if you plan to deliver less content to your mobile user, chances are your CMS isn't going to make that easy on you. You're still going to have to maintain two versions of that content, and update them separately whenever there's a change.

In other words, you're forked.

Responsive design to the rescue?

Responsive design is often held up as a solution that saves you from having to maintain multiple separate codebases for your front-end code. Put the effort in to developing one set of code that will adapt to different screen sizes and progressively enhance for different device capabilities, and you'll save time in the long run. You'll also get out of the arms race of having to support dozens of different devices and form factors.

Responsive design is also an approach that saves you from forking your content. If you have a coupled CMS that can only handle publishing to one set of templates, then you can trick your CMS into publishing to different devices by handling the conversion to mobile or tablet sizes on the front-end.

But responsive design is just one tactic that may help solve this problem. The decision on whether to develop a responsive site or to maintain different templates for desktop, phone, and everything in-between is a pragmatic choice based on how you want to allocate time and resources for development and maintenance. There are good reasons for both approaches—often rooted in the specifics of how your CMS functions—and what works for one organization may not work for another.

Whether you choose to employ a responsive design or opt to develop separate templates for different screen sizes, there is still an underlying issue that needs to be solved. Let's not lose sight of the fundamental issue, which is how to evolve our content management tools and processes to effectively support multi-channel publishing.

DON'T GET FORKED IN THE APP

The CEO of BigCo got an iPad on the day it came out. (He's got friends in Cupertino.) He loves his new toy. He loves it so much, in fact, that he wants to give iPads to his entire salesforce. He imagines the tablet will be a great sales tool—more intimate than a presentation given in a dark conference room by the light of the projector and less awkward than having prospective clients huddle around a laptop. Also? Way cooler.

He gives his team a mandate: he wants the salesforce outfitted with iPads that they'll use to demo products by the end of the year. He's not alone in this ambition. Seventy-eight percent of enterprises surveyed by Model Metrics say they plan to deploy tablets by the end of 2013, and forty-seven percent of them say they want to use tablets as tools for their salesforce (http://bkaprt.com/csm/37; PDF).

The digital team started brainstorming how their native iPad app should look and work. Excited about the possibilities, they imagined interactive graphics showing schematic product diagrams, video demos, even product spec sheets that can be customized on the fly. And, of course, all the slick motion transitions and gestural behaviors that come along with a native iOS app.

Exciting, right? "Hold on there, guys," the lone content strategist said, "I have a few questions." Questions like:

- Are we going to repurpose the product information from the desktop website for this app, or do we need to create all new content?
- What about the videos and interactive graphics? Those don't exist today—are we going to create all of them? Creating new videos and graphics will be expensive, so shouldn't we have a plan to put them up on the desktop website too?
- Is all this content going to live in our current CMS? What will be the process to publish content from the CMS to the iPad app? If we're creating different content for the desktop website and the iPad, will the CMS make it possible to manage that content as one integrated package?
- What if the CMS won't play nicely with the iPad app? Will we need to migrate a chunk of the content to live in the app?
- If we're maintaining two completely separate versions of our product content, what will happen when we update the product information, or when we launch a new product? How will we keep the website and the iPad app in sync?
- Are you going to double my salary now that I'm doing twice the work?

These examples aren't mere hypotheticals. Great ideas for mobile experiences—carried out by successful companies with the resources and budget to develop them—can fail if they haven't figured out the workflow needed to support and maintain them.

DON'T DOUBLE YOUR WORKLOAD

Imagine you visited the Gap's website on your laptop computer one day this spring. You might have been enticed to buy a spring raincoat, or maybe even try this season's hottest trend, neon denim trousers. (Or maybe not.) Had you visited the mobile website on the very same day, you would have felt a chill in the air from all the winter clothes on that homepage (FIG 2.1).

Looking at the disparity between these two sites, you might wonder if Colin, the junior marketing guy in charge of

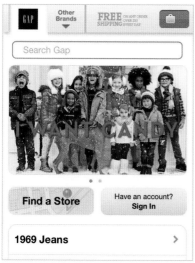

FIG 2.1: Spring has sprung on the Gap's desktop website. Too bad someone forgot to tell those poor shivering kids over on the mobile site.

updating the mobile website, got fired over this boneheaded mistake. Looking at this problem across an entire industry, however, you realize the solution isn't blaming the low man on the totem pole. The Gap's problem isn't Colin. The Gap's problem is that they have two completely separate processes for maintaining each homepage—maybe even two distinct systems, operated by two different people. Instead of updating the new homepage graphic in *one* place and having it automatically publish to everywhere it needs to go, they forked their content.

Even though they have processes that encourage this kind of inconsistency, the Gap still wants to communicate the same messages to the same customers. (It's not like they realized that all their mobile users live in the frozen tundra, right?)

American Eagle pulls this off by not forking their content. They maintain one set of content—they use the same homepage image everywhere, even though it might be cropped and laid out differently for different screen sizes (**FIG 2.2**). This means they can communicate one consistent message across the desktop, mobile web, and mobile app. Their process and workflow is simplified, because they only have to update the content in one place. (Or maybe their version of Colin is just way more on the ball.)

More work in your workflow

Since 2010, magazine publisher Condé Nast has invested heavily in building custom iPad editions for some of its most popular titles, including *Glamour, GQ, Wired,* and *Vanity Fair.* Existing art and production staffers have doubled—no, tripled—their workload, first laying out the print edition, then repurposing its design and content for two different iPad layouts: portrait and landscape (http://bkaprt.com/csm/38).

These iPad editions are not so much a digital magazine as a giant PDF of the print edition. As such they lack many of the benefits you might expect from a truly digital property:

FIG 2.2: American Eagle pulls off a hat trick: consistent content and messaging across desktop web, mobile web, and iOS app.

They're heavy

Digital magazines regularly weigh in at 150 MB or more, taking twenty minutes to download on a broadband connection. You could drive to the store and buy the print magazine in less time (http://bkaprt.com/csm/39).

They're unsociable

Want to send one of your friends a link to an article? Copy and paste some of the text to quote on your blog? Heck, do you want to search the text? These basic digital functions are made cumbersome—or impossible—by the fact that what you're looking at is a giant picture of the print magazine.

They're gimmicky

The print editorial teams behind most iPad editions don't want to seem like they've missed the interactive revolution. The content gets dressed up with unnecessary animations and glitzy transitions that don't necessarily add value for the iPad reader. This problem is magnified because the effort that goes into creating these effects doesn't benefit anyone else—they're tablet only.

They're not earning their keep

We could overlook this if digital magazines were delivering real value to readers and the business. They're not. Let's take Condé Nast's *Glamour* magazine as an example. *Glamour* is known in the industry for being Condé's most lucrative title. In the U.S. they sell more than two million annual print subscriptions. glamour.com has an online monthly readership of about 1.2 million unique visitors. Yet in November 2010, they sold 2,775 copies of the iPad edition. Can you imagine being the beleaguered *Glamour* magazine staffer who has to stay up nights and work weekends after the print magazine has gone to bed, laying out *two* different versions of an iPad edition that sells fewer than 3,000 copies?

The core problem here isn't that sales are weak, or that iPad editions don't live up to what we expect in digital. The problem is that Condé Nast has created much more work for themselves, and they aren't seeing a return on that investment. Scott Dadich, Condé Nast's Content Innovation VP— and the architect of their iPad strategy—acknowledged that the problem is their workflow: "Bringing it all together into a cohesive workflow has been a real challenge for us. It's been tough—there's a lot more work" (http://bkaprt.com/csm/40).

NO FORKING WAY

The acrimony and the debates around mobile web *vs.* native apps, or responsive design *vs.* separate templates are missing the point. The challenge for most organizations in the long run won't be figuring out a development approach for cross-platform code—because these techniques will evolve and standardize.

The challenge will be supporting a multi-channel editorial workflow, particularly if they want to prioritize content differently across platforms.

Any arguments about whether to deliver less content or different content to the mobile users need to consider the effort required to manage and maintain that content. If you're going around suggesting that you want to provide a different experience for mobile users, or you want to cut content from the mobile website, be aware that this approach may doom you to content maintenance and governance headaches. Paying attention to this is the very essence of content strategy.

The root of the problem is in our internal processes, workflow, and tools. To avoid the problem of content forking we need a new approach to publishing content to multiple devices. We need adaptive content.

THE FUTURE IS ADAPTIVE CONTENT

Let's say we all agree on a glorious future, in which desktop and mobile users all get access to complete (or at least, equivalent) content, appropriately structured, designed, and formatted for their device. Whether we want to deliver exactly the same content to everyone, or prioritize and feature content differently on different platforms, we have a process that helps us do that without wasted effort. That future is *adaptive content*. Adaptive content is content that is flexible, so it can adapt to different screen sizes, and can be presented in different formats as appropriate for the device. What's the secret to this flexibility? Why, it's having more structure! Adaptive content has structure and metadata attached to it, which helps it figure out what to do when it winds up on all those different platforms and devices.

Adaptive content is composed of these five elements:

- Content that gets created with the goal of making it reusable, rather than by someone who imagines that it will "live" on a particular platform.
- Structured content that can be combined in different ways for different platforms.
- Presentation-independent content that hasn't been styled and formatted for a single display.
- Metadata that will allow platforms to "query" the content and display the content elements best suited to a particular display.
- A CMS user interface that encourages writers to create content elements and variations within a package, instead of tying content to specific pages.

Understanding adaptive content is super important to developing your content strategy for mobile. Let's dig into this topic in more detail in the next chapter.

3
ADAPTIVE CONTENT

"Get your content ready to go anywhere because it's going to go everywhere."
—**BRAD FROST** (http://bkaprt.com/csm/41)

Adaptive content is more than just "mobile." It means getting your content into a format so you can share and distribute it to any platform you want. It means you can get your content onto platforms you control—and platforms you don't. It even means you'll have a fighting shot at getting your content onto platforms that haven't been invented yet.

Rich Ziade, CEO of Readability, told me that he thinks this problem is even bigger than mobile:

> The mobile browser is no longer the sole destination of the hyperlink. Stuff opens inside of Twitter, Facebook, etc., and that means that content needs to be ready to go in all these new contexts. Content is being plucked and refitted everywhere. Take a look at most modern Twitter clients: they show Instagram

photos and links to videos inline in the Tweet. That's not a
webpage anymore. It's just the content in whatever context
makes sense. *This is one step beyond responsive design and form*
factors of devices. It is content reduced down to its essence then
custom-tailored.

The magic trick we're trying to perform is to get our content ready to go anywhere. Smartphones might be the most pressing multi-platform problem right now, but they're not going to be the last one. Can you imagine your content showing up on someone's heads-up display, like Google Goggles? Being read aloud during someone's commute to work? Appearing (and being readable) across the room, on someone's giant-screen TV set?

Noz Urbina from Mekon, Ltd. told me he wonders whether our content is ready to go into the kitchen:

> *What happens when your cooktop functions like a giant*
> *iPad? Manufacturers are already making noise on the internet*
> *about data-enabling various household devices, and how*
> *resistant they will be to extremes of temperature and shock.*
> *Will your content be ready to go there? It's a great content*
> *consumption context.*

What would it look like if you thought of your content as a service that could be accessed by a variety of different platforms, rather than as a substance that lives in a particular location?

CONTENT AS A SERVICE

NPR, America's National Public Radio, has spent several years making their content accessible through an approach they call COPE, which stands for Create Once, Publish Everywhere. As a result, they have a clean base of well-structured content that they can display on many platforms.

A book review that includes a headline, teaser content, body copy, audio, multiple images, topic categorization, and book metadata can be displayed on a wide variety of

FIG 3.1: The NPR.org website includes the headline, body text of the story, the audio file, one image, and book metadata (http://bkaprt.com/csm/42).

platforms. Each platform can choose which content objects it wants to display, and how to format them (FIG 3.1-3.5).

These examples from NPR illustrate two key aspects of adaptive content: multiple content structures and tailored visual presentation.

Multiple content structures

NPR writes a summary for each piece, which means that their story gets an appropriate introduction, wherever it might appear. While other publications might think they could just rely on the first sentence or two of the article to serve as a teaser, NPR takes the time to write a custom summary. They don't just write one teaser, either: they write two! A short version

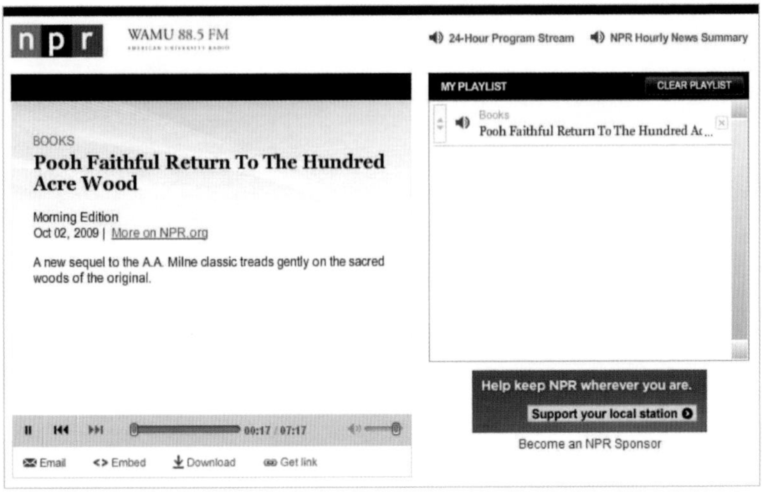

FIG 3.2: The NPR.org audio player displays the headline, the short summary, and the audio file. Note that the audio player functionality looks and works differently in this version than on the main NPR.org website.

and a long version gives them extra flexibility, allowing each platform to decide how much space to devote to the summary.

Another interesting way that NPR uses multiple content structures is that they treat the body copy for the story and the audio file like they're equal—neither is considered primary. Whether the platform is more text-focused (like a website) or more audio-focused (like a player) each content package can be displayed for maximum effect. Each platform can choose the right mix of content objects—teasers, audio, and images can be combined in different ways based on what each platform needs and does well.

While NPR only creates one headline for each story, it's possible that they could write more. If you're thinking about creating multiple content structures, writing multiple headlines also offers more flexibility. You could write shorter and longer versions, some optimized for SEO, some for human consumption. (We'll cover how to do this in the chapter on information architecture.)

FIG 3.3: Here's the exact same story as it appears in the iTunes desktop application. It shows the headline, the long summary, and the audio file.

Unique visual presentation

If you care about providing great design and a user experience that's appropriate for a given platform, you need to be thinking about adaptive content.

NPR has the ability to make the same story look and function differently on each platform. The order, density, and priority of content is different. The typography is different. The use of images is different. The audio player is different. Even though each platform draws from the exact same content package, they all look and feel like their own unique experience. They can tailor the design to create the best experience for that platform.

This is possible because NPR focuses on creating structured content independent of visual presentation. They

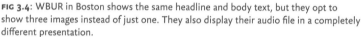
FIG 3.4: WBUR in Boston shows the same headline and body text, but they opt to show three images instead of just one. They also display their audio file in a completely different presentation.

permit and enable each delivery platform to make its own decisions about how to style the content, because formatting isn't embedded in the content. They also create content for maximum flexibility, creating multiple sizes and versions for text, images, and audio formats. And, they make it possible for each platform to query the content to determine which content chunks to display.

As a result, each platform can deliver a great user experience, tailored for the capabilities of each device.

How do they do it?

How does this magic happen? And is it something you can do in your organization, even if you're not a major publisher like NPR? You can, if you start thinking about creating adaptive content.

Getting there means you need to create content that embodies the five key elements of adaptive content:

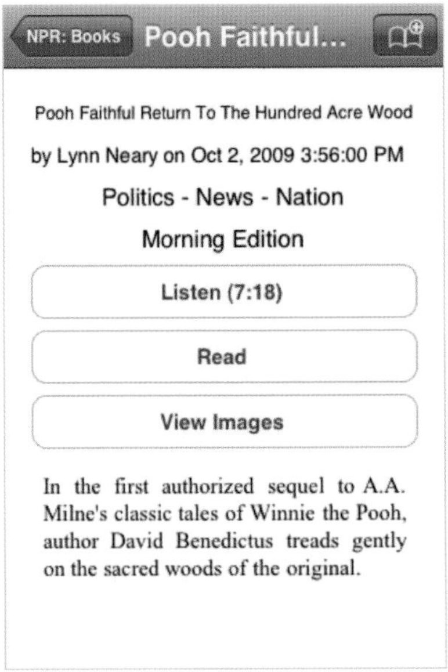

Pooh Faithful...

Pooh Faithful Return To The Hundred Acre Wood

by Lynn Neary on Oct 2, 2009 3:56:00 PM

Politics - News - Nation

Morning Edition

Listen (7:18)

Read

View Images

In the first authorized sequel to A.A. Milne's classic tales of Winnie the Pooh, author David Benedictus treads gently on the sacred woods of the original.

FIG 3.5: The NPR mobile app shows the same story and content elements, but with a very different presentation of the headline, long summary, audio file, body text, and images (http://bkaprt.com/csm/42).

- **Reusable content:** content has been developed to maximize reuse across platforms; where that's impossible, different formats or types of content are available.
- **Structured content:** discrete content chunks can be combined in different ways for different platforms.
- **Presentation-independent content:** design decisions can be made by the platform, rather than having style and format imposed on the content.
- **Meaningful metadata:** category, tag, author, and date information can be used to filter or highlight content, and metadata can be used to help platforms decide which content to display.
- **Usable CMS interfaces:** content management UI and workflow encourages people to create well-structured and metadata-enhanced content, without letting them fall back on making styling choices.

Let's look at each of these in turn.

REUSABLE CONTENT

If you're thinking of a specific context when you create content, your mind naturally wraps itself into the opportunities and constraints inherent in that medium. Imagining that your content can and will be reused in many ways poses its own set of limitations and benefits.

While many things need to change before organizations can start creating reusable content, the most fundamental challenge is a change in mindset. Content creators need to break free of imagining a single context where their content is going to "live" and instead plan for content reuse.

Written for reuse

Content written for one context often doesn't make the leap to other places all that well. To give your content the best shot at making sense in whatever way the user wants or needs to consume it, you should do the following:

Write standalone headlines

Because you can use page titles in multiple places, write standalone headlines so that they can serve as page headers and links. If you're only going to write one page title, then ensure that headline includes keywords to help the user decide whether she wants to click on the link, and determine if she's in the right place.

The following headlines are used for both the article title and the link title on landing pages and in search engines. They offer keywords and an enticement to click (http://bkaprt.com/csm/43):

- 15 Case Studies to Get Your Client on Board With Social Media (*Mashable,* http://bkaprt.com/csm/44)
- Scott Forstall, the Sorcerer's Apprentice at Apple (*Bloomberg Businessweek,* http://bkaprt.com/csm/45)
- What Everyone Is Too Polite to Say About Steve Jobs (*Gawker,* http://bkaprt.com/csm/46)

Write multiple headlines

Sometimes, it's just not possible to write a single headline that works in every context. You may have to write multiple headline versions—some that work as page titles, some that work as links. (More about how to do this is coming up, in the chapter on information architecture.)

The following headlines offer a good balance—headlines that work as entertaining page titles aren't expected to do double-duty as links (http://bkaprt.com/csm/43). This approach provides extra value when combined in a one-two punch— they could be combined into a longer headline or the link title could be used as a summary:

- Article Title: "What's Eating the NYPD?"; link: Why the NYPD Is Turning on Ray Kelly (*New York Magazine,* http://bkaprt.com/csm/47)
- Article Title: "Citizen Cain"; link: Herman Cain's Unlikely Republican Rise (*Newsweek,* http://bkaprt.com/csm/48)
- Article Title: "When Is a Flip Not a Flop?"; link: The Fate of the Republicans Who Supported Gay Marriage (*The New York Times Magazine,* http://bkaprt.com/csm/49)

Don't bury the lede

When you write for the web, put the most important information up front. If you don't grab your reader right from the start, they're likely to wander off in search of something more interesting.

This adage is even more true when you're writing content that may be reused in other contexts. If the first sentence/paragraph contain meaty, useful information, you protect yourself if they ever need to be used as a navigation summary or if the rest of the text gets truncated. If the first sentence says nothing of interest, why would your reader want to tap for more information?

Similarly, you should focus on just one main idea in each chunk of text (whether that's a paragraph or a section).

Readers are likely to scan headings and initial sentences, searching for words that they think will answer their questions. If you combine multiple ideas in a chunk with no visual separation or distinction between them, important information will likely be overlooked.

Alternative content

One of the most frustrating parts of looking at content on mobile devices is discovering that useful or necessary content isn't accessible because the content format didn't translate well to a different screen size or platform capability. Whether it's a video that's only available in Flash, or an infographic that doesn't scale for a smaller screen, some content just won't work in other contexts.

Creating reusable content means recognizing when content *can't* be reused, and developing an alternative. Remember how NPR could publish the same story to a website and an audio player? Having both text and audio gives them more options. You might need to consider alternatives for the following:

Images

Scaling images and infographics across a tiny mobile phone and a giant Retina display just won't work. You will need additional image sizes cropped. If the image can't be cropped or scaled without losing its meaning, then you will need an alternative: find another image or describe the image's content in the body text or alt text.

Data visualizations

Interactive data visualizations can be engaging both on the desktop and on touchscreens, provided they're built for reuse across platforms. In situations where the screen size or device capabilities won't support their display, have a fallback mechanism, like displaying a simple table of the data.

Audio and video

Alternative formats (taking advantage of HTML5's support for multiple video formats) will help ensure that everyone can access these forms of media. Beyond that, providing a transcript or text summary for any audio or video content will make it more flexible for reuse (as well as more accessible to people with disabilities and friendly to search engines).

Managed reuse

Have you ever searched around in your email, Word documents, or website, looking for a snippet of content you'd previously created and wanted to reuse? Across a variety of different forms of professional communication—cover letters, business proposals, legal documents—it doesn't make sense to keep creating and recreating the wheel.

Most people handle this process opportunistically: they hunt around for the paragraph or graphic they want to repurpose, then copy and paste it into place. Others might handle it in a more organized fashion, maintaining a library of boilerplate documents that they can efficiently browse or search.

But what most people don't have is a system that manages content for planned reuse. Because you're copying and pasting each content element uniquely, you're creating different instances of the content. If you want to make a change to that content object, you'll have to change it everywhere you used it.

That might work for your individual publishing workflow, but it's not going to fly when you're planning for large-scale, multi-channel publishing. Effective content reuse across platforms means you need a way to update content in one place and have the changes reflected everywhere.

To support that, you'll need the next aspect of adaptive content, which is **structured content**.

STRUCTURED CONTENT

"The more structure you put into content the freer it will become."
—RACHEL LOVINGER, Content Strategy Director, Razorfish
(http://bkaprt.com/csm/50; PDF)

The foundation of adaptive content is structured content: to make content flexible for reuse, you must structure it into meaningful chunks.

Structured content is fundamental to how we think about publishing on the internet. Instead of being fixed on paper, content is stored in a database. The structure we put into that database gives content more meaning, which means we can do more with it. If we break long stretches of content down into smaller chunks, we're then free to combine and recombine them in new ways. If we categorize our content consistently—either by entering it into fields or marking it up with tags—then we can sort, filter, and prioritize it.

None of this happens by magic. It takes human effort (and/or really smart robots) to add the right structure to content. And because it takes effort, it's easy to backslide.

Chunks, not blobs

Many organizations insist their editing workflow requires a giant blob into which they can dump whatever they want—text, headings, images, tables, audio, videos—anything and everything that can show up on a webpage. If your organization is using a blogging platform like WordPress as its CMS, you know what this looks like. Content creators get one big field for the body of their content, and it's like their own personal playground (**FIG 3.6**).

What happens to that giant blob of stuff (that's the technical term) when it's time to put it on another platform? Your content can't be broken up into smaller pieces for display and reading on different screens. Your content can't be targeted differently to different platforms—forget about an NPR-style COPE model, or even alternatives for unsupported content

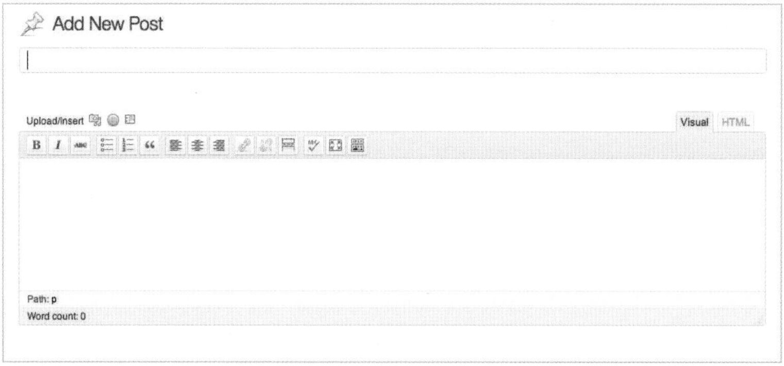

FIG 3.6: WordPress was originally designed as a blogging platform. Its primary input mechanism is an unstructured blob.

types. Your content blob will gloppily resist any attempt to make it firm up.

If you want your content to be reusable, flexible, and adaptable to change, it needs structure.

Tumblr takes a totally different approach to a content editing workflow, guiding users to create appropriate chunks of content, rather than just giving them one big blob. Tumblr defines a set of content types: photos, quotes, chat transcripts, audio, video, and links, in addition to the generic text blob.

Different interfaces for each of these content types help guide users to structure their content. Because Tumblr took the time to figure out which fields and metadata would be required to support each content type, they can help users enter their information more easily. Done well, structured content makes for a better editing experience for content authors (FIG 3.7–3.8).

The war of blobs vs. chunks comes down to having strong content structure. But how do you achieve that? In the same way that Tumblr defined a set of content types (photo, quote, audio) and defined the fields that would make up those types, you need to figure out how to structure your content.

This process of defining what your content is and how to chunk it up in your database is called *content modeling*.

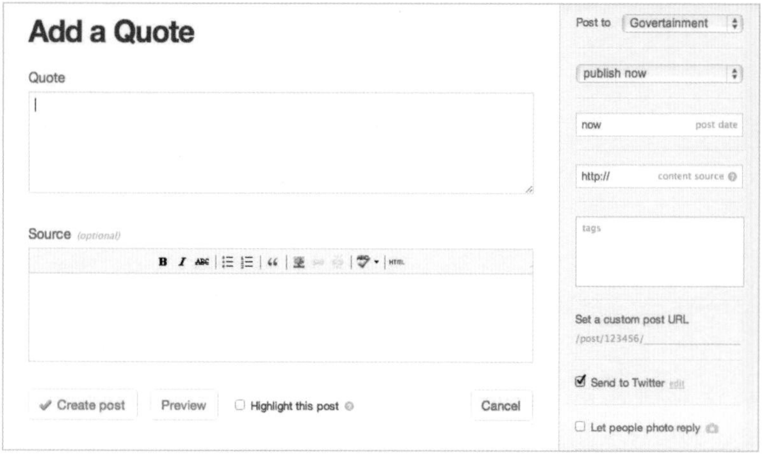

FIG 3.7: A quote could be handled in a generic text blob. But by defining it as its own content type, with specific fields for the quote and the source, Tumblr can display quotes differently on the front-end.

Content modeling

For most content management platforms, this means having properly "fielded" content chunks. Discrete content elements are broken out into different fields in the interface and the database, which means these chunks can be combined in different ways on different platforms.

The process by which these content chunks get defined is called content modeling. Modeling is the way you turn all your undifferentiated blobs of content into a defined, organized system of:

- **Content types:** what kind of content is it? Is it an article, product spec, recipe, slideshow, etc.?
- **Attributes:** what fields or content elements can or must be entered? Does the content include headings, body text, images, audio files, author name, or author bio?
- **Data limits:** what limits are set on each attribute? Does the field require a specific numeric format, image specification, character limit, or date format?

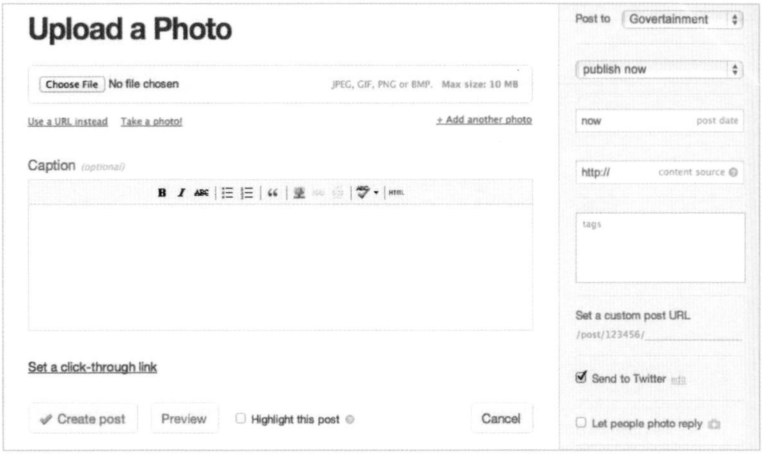

Upload a Photo

Choose File No file chosen   JPEG, GIF, PNG or BMP. Max size: 10 MB

Use a URL instead   Take a photo!   + Add another photo

Caption (optional)

B I ABC | ≡ ≡ | 66 | ⬛ ⬛ ⬛ | ✎ ▾ | HTML.

Set a click-through link

✓ Create post   Preview   ☐ Highlight this post ⊙   Cancel

Post to Govertainment ⬍

publish now ⬍

now   post date

http://   content source ⊙

tags

Set a custom post URL
/post/123456/

☑ Send to Twitter edit

☐ Let people photo reply

FIG 3.8: Note that the input mechanism to upload a photo guides the user, whether she wants to choose a file, select a URL, or take a photo with her camera. Note also that Tumblr decided that a title field wasn't necessary for the photo content type.

- **Relationships:** how are different content types connected? What attributes and data limits can be shared among different content types?

Content modeling in action

Tech Guy Labs is a nationally-syndicated radio show call-in show. Their website (http://bkaprt.com/csm/51) was at one time based on a simple wiki. But because all their content— names of guests, lists of questions, and episode videos—was stored in giant blobs, the site was nearly unusable. It couldn't be searched. It was painful to use on mobile devices. And forget about trying to repurpose this valuable content in new ways.

A recent redesign reorganized the site around the episode as a central concept. The content model defined the episode as the primary content type, with different content types for

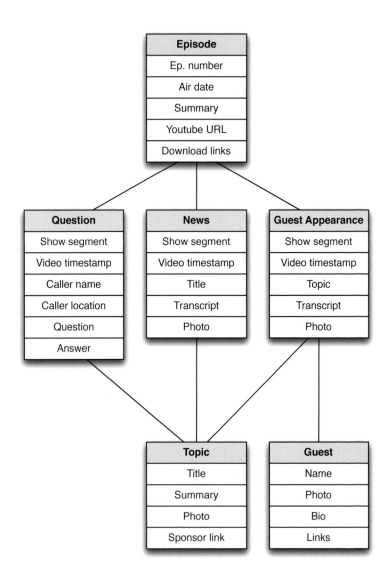

FIG 3.9: This diagram shows the content types (in gray) and the content attributes (in white) for the radio call-in show, Tech Guy Labs. The primary content type is an episode, and each episode has segments. Segments all share information about topics.

each segment of the show—a guest appearance has a different structure and different attributes from a question segment (**FIG 3.9**).

This content model asks users to apply more structure than they did when using a wiki, but they get more value from the content. The website can be more easily browsed—adding metadata that calls out topics or guest names means that users can find what they're looking for more easily.

Jeff Eaton, Senior Architect at Lullabot, who led the redesign, told me that this content model's value goes beyond making the website more browsable:

Now that they've bitten the bullet and migrated their content to a richer, more descriptive schema, a world of possibilities have opened for them. The idea of a custom smartphone application to listen to episodes was previously a pipe dream, but now it could pull from the same underlying stream of content as their website. Caller questions are now "geocoded" with location information, rather than simply having the name of a city floating somewhere in the text of the transcript— allowing them to build interactive maps to show off their broad base of listeners. And highlighting "best questions of the week" and other promotional content is as simple as flagging one article or another, not an arduous exercise in creating entirely new material.

Content modeling in the CMS

Rather than just dumping all their content into one big blob, ask users to enter it into discrete fields in the CMS (**FIG 3.10**).

But make no mistake: the content model is bigger than the CMS interface that supports it. The content model needs to reflect the needs and goals of the content authors who will create content (not to mention the people who will read the content).

Creating structured content within a content model means making a leap: you're writing content for the chunk and not for the page.

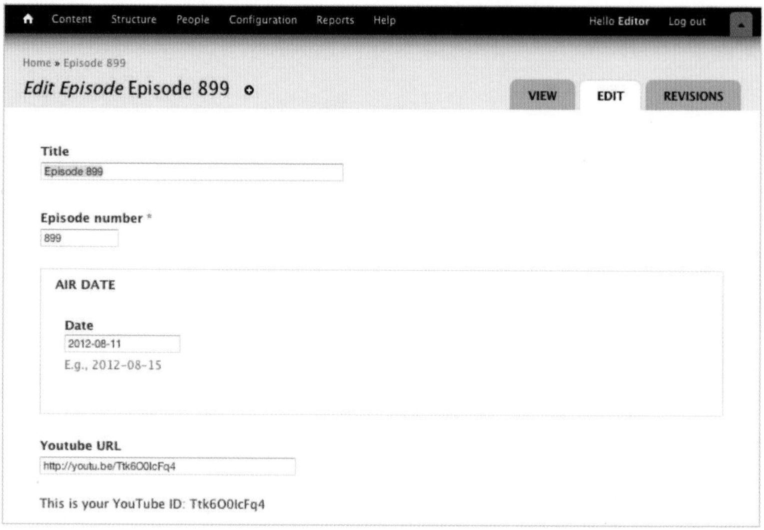

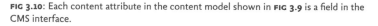

Content
Structure
People
Configuration
Reports
Help
Hello Editor
Log out
Home » Episode 899
Edit Episode Episode 899
VIEW
EDIT
REVISIONS
Title
Episode 899
Episode number *
899
AIR DATE
Date
2012-08-11
E.g., 2012-08-15
Youtube URL
http://youtu.be/Ttk6O0lcFq4
This is your YouTube ID: Ttk6O0lcFq4

FIG 3.10: Each content attribute in the content model shown in **FIG 3.9** is a field in the CMS interface.

Packages, not pages

Your content strategy for mobile shouldn't involve creating content that will live on only one platform. That doesn't mean, however, that you must publish *exactly* the same content to every single platform. With adaptive content, your goal is to create a flexible base of content with a variety of structured content objects to cover a wide range of uses and contexts.

So what's the difference between creating content for each platform, and creating multiple content structures? In both cases, you're writing more content, right?

The difference is that a content strategy for mobile means you're creating *content packages.* If you're thinking of developing multiple content structures within a single, discrete package, you're planning ahead to make it easier to create, maintain, and govern content. Instead of having forked content and separate workflows, you manage and maintain a package of content all in one place.

Do you need multiple versions of headlines? Shorter and longer summaries? Alternative versions of graphics, tables, or videos? Creating, managing, and maintaining all this content is much easier if you think of it as a single discrete package with a set of different content objects, rather than as separate workflows leading to separate websites.

Responsive content

The worst case scenario is to force mobile devices to load all the available content over expensive data plans, then hide it or truncate it to fit in the designs. Unfortunately, for most current implementations of mobile content, that's the best we can do when all we can control is the front-end.

Responsive web design advocates have jumped to advocating for responsive content: content that can automagically reformat itself for different screen sizes or platforms, dynamically showing more or less content according to what the interface, device capability, bandwidth, or user context can support.

Two things are required to deliver on this notion of responsive content. First, it has to be structured as we're describing here: broken up into appropriate chunks, with meaningful metadata and useful business rules attached.

But structured content is only one aspect of responsive content. As Mark Boulton, Creative Director at Mark Boulton Design, explains, without the right design system to make sense of the content, the content is still just a static object (http://bkaprt.com/csm/52):

> *Content that travels around with a set of rules or metadata that will allow responsive design systems to make good use of them. But this does not make this content responsive. On its own, it's pretty dumb: just floating around with additional information attached to it, until some smart design system grabs it and displays in the right context.*

Unless both of those conditions are met, responsive content just isn't a thing. If we agree that the ideal scenario is a world where we can display content differently according to different device needs or context constraints, then we have some work to do to get there. If that's your goal, then it's time to invest in developing structured content. Structured content is the foundation of adaptive content. It goes hand-in-hand with a third attribute, which is that the content must be **independent from its presentation.**

PRESENTATION-INDEPENDENT CONTENT

"Metadata is the new art direction."
—ETHAN RESNICK, design student at New York University (Quipped over a really interesting dinner conversation.)

Every platform is unique. What works for print doesn't necessarily carry over to the web. Mobile web and desktop web require different design conventions. User interface design for iOS isn't the same as on Android.

If you want to provide a great user experience for a given platform, you can't just repurpose a design intended for another platform. If your content inherits layout, formatting, and styling intended for one device, you're going to have to strip it out and start over when you send your content to a different device. The problem is, those design choices tell you about the *meaning* of the content.

A better way is to separate content from presentation right from the start, and ensure that the meaning of the content isn't described only by how it looks.

Separation of content from form

On the web, everyone's a designer. Content authors insist that they need to control how their content is styled. They demand the ability to alter the page layout, choose different fonts and colors, and choose the exact placement of images on the page. When they're done, the page looks great—in the one and only one context they were imagining when they created it, which was the desktop web.

This problem runs deep. Our legacy of print publishing gives us five hundred years of precedent that content and form are inextricably intertwined. It's nearly impossible for some content authors to imagine what they want to say separate from how it looks.

As a result, we've baked this assumption into our content management tools. Content creators demand the ability to style their text, and so we give it to them—at the expense of reusable content, says information architect Rick Yagodich (http://bkaprt.com/csm/53):

> Too many CMSs provide rich text formatting—the ability for the author to identify presentation control directly within a block of text; the inclusion and placement of images; the styling of paragraphs; the specification of link targets—to have any claim to separating content from presentation. If an element of content is to be reusable—say rendered onto a website, into a print publication, through a mobile app, accessed via an API feed—it must exist in a form other than pre-formatted HTML. The element needs to be clean, a self-contained value.

You see rich text formatting in the familiar toolbar at the top of every content entry screen.

Beware the WYSIWYG toolbar

"Make it work just like Microsoft Word!" It's a rallying cry to return to a simpler era, an attempt to make content on the web seem as controlled and predictable as putting ink on paper (FIG 3.11).

The best evidence that we're crossing our fingers and hoping we can make the web more like print is the WYSIWYG toolbar. "What you see is what you get" is a vestige of the desktop publishing revolution, made possible by having screen displays optimized for a particular type of output. For Microsoft Word and other desktop publishing tools, that's the laser printer next to your desk. For your CMS, that's your desktop website. Oops.

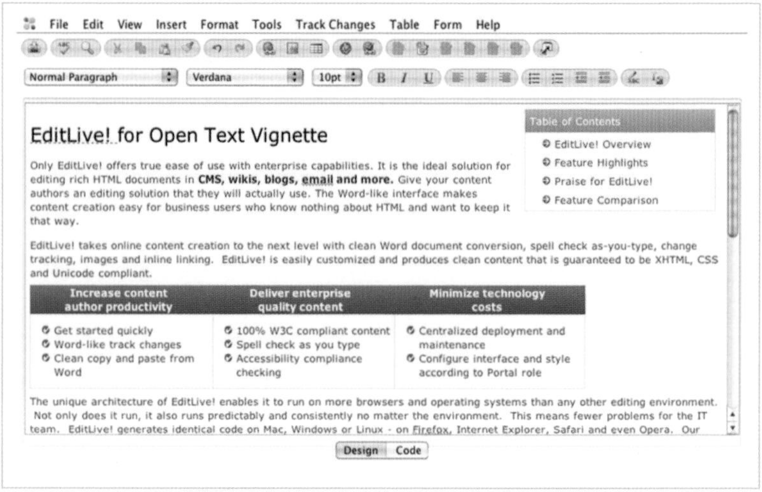

FIG 3.11: Saying your CMS offers a "Word-like" interface makes it seem like you think the web is print. What happens to all that formatting when you want to display this content on mobile?

WYSIWYG is problematic because it encourages CMS users to embed formatting in with their content, allowing them to imagine that their designs will display beautifully—on the desktop. When it's time to publish these pages onto mobile devices, all this extraneous formatting needs to be stripped out so the content displays appropriately on different screen sizes. All that effort, all that meaning encoded in visual styling—lost.

Trying to control layout and styling for a particular output is a thing of the past, says web developer Eoin Kelly (http://bkaprt.com/csm/54):

The whole notion of WYSIWYG makes perfect sense if you are creating a document that is destined to be frozen as a PDF or on paper. However, on the web a WYSIWYG is a thin veneer of "Word Processor" sanity over HTML and CSS. Not only does HTML and CSS not make it easy to have precise, repeatable control over layout—they deliberately make it difficult. Why? It turns out that variable layout is generally a good thing. It defers decisions about how content should be presented to devices that are closer to the end user, the assumption being that the device knows better than we do how to present the content to the user.

Content structure expressed through styling

A related—but different—problem is that tools offered by a typical CMS conflate structure with styling. When we publish our content, what it means is often encoded by defining *how it looks* or *where it lives*.

At the field level

Many times, we encode structural information merely through styling. Data like author names or movie titles or calendar dates get pasted into the body of the text, perhaps formatted in bold or italics. But just because those text elements have been styled visually doesn't mean you can do anything with them. If that metadata were called out separately—stored in a unique field in the database, or marked up with semantic tags that describe what the content means (rather than just how it should be styled)—it would be more useful and more actionable.

In the late 1980s, *TV Guide* was the most popular magazine in America. They might have patted themselves on the back, secure in their position as the most successful magazine publisher.

But they didn't stop there. They realized that they weren't in the magazine publishing business—they were in the *content publishing* business. They split the company in two: one division to manage the magazine brand, and another division that owned the database of program content.

Then, they built a green-screen, mainframe application, and told their writers that going forward, they'd be entering all their content into this tool. Creating a database for their content gave it more value. Entering show titles and genres as separate fields in the database gave them valuable

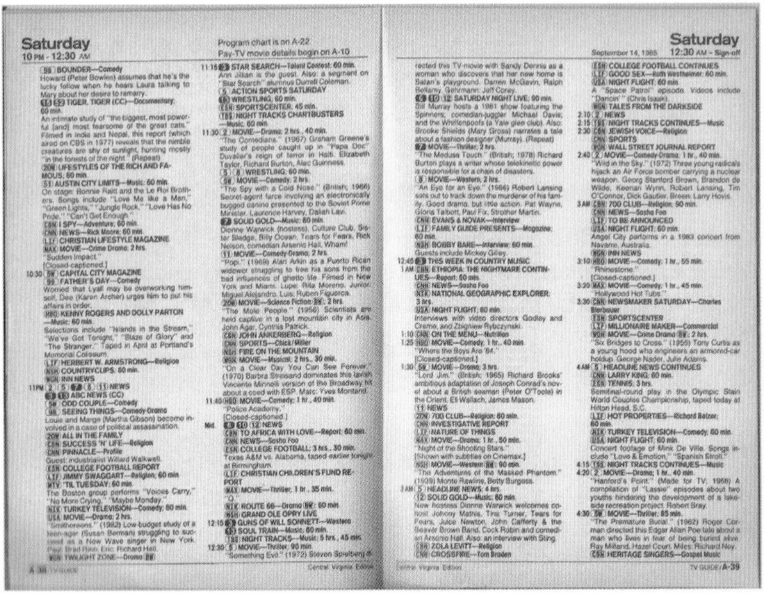

FIG 3.12: Show titles and categories aren't just "bold" or "all caps" formatting—they're valuable metadata. (Thanks to Dan Saffer for the example. http://bkaprt.com/csm/56)

metadata— they could search and filter on those categories in a way that would be impossible in print (FIG 3.12). They even asked their writers to develop *three* different summaries for each program, which gave them more flexibility in where that content could live in the future.

In 2008, the assets of the division that owned the *TV Guide* magazine brand were sold for $1 (http://bkaprt.com/csm/55). One dollar! Less than the cost of a single issue on the newsstand to purchase the entire publication's assets. That's because there was no value in the printed magazine. All the value in that company was contained in the structured content assets held in their database.

At the page level

Structural information also gets encoded through layout. When news editors want to communicate to readers which stories they think are most important, they make decisions about the layout of homepages and section fronts, making some stories more visible and others less prominent. A glance at any newspaper front page will give you a sense of the visual cues at our disposal: placement of the story; column inches devoted to the story; headline type size; use of bold, italics, or all caps; number of subheads; and the size of the images.

Web editors, constrained by the templating system baked into their CMS, have fewer controls available—often, they encode the importance of the story solely through its placement on the page, and the style sheet takes care of choices about typography and sizing.

Defining structure and priority through visual styles and positioning works great when—say it with me now—you expect your content to live on one and only one platform.

What happens to all that valuable editorial decision making when the layout of the homepage changes? When editors rearrange their homepage, all that data, all that insight is *lost*. The judgement about the importance of a given story was attached to the layout of the homepage, not to the story itself. Update the page layout, lose the editorial perspective.

The Guardian recognized that all the valuable editorial judgement that went into laying out the print edition was being lost on other platforms. How could they preserve that so it could inform the iPad version? Robots to the rescue! They developed an algorithm that reads the original InDesign files from the print edition, studying the size and placement of each article to calculate the article's priority. The iPad version uses that data to make its own decisions about where to place articles within the app (http://bkaprt.com/csm/57; **FIG 3.13**).

Now, not every organization will be able to write complex algorithms that read their print layouts—an innovative approach by *The Guardian* isn't a long-term solution for most

FIG 3.13: *The Guardian* developed an algorithm to read the print homepage and turn its layout into metadata that the iPad uses to automatically generate its own layout.

organizations. The lesson to take away from this example isn't that robots will rescue us from print-centric styling. Rather, you should think about how best to encode your content with *meaning*, rather than just styling.

So, if we can't encode what the content means through visual presentation, how do we do it? That brings us to the fourth aspect of adaptive content, **meaningful metadata.**

MEANINGFUL METADATA

"Metadata is a love note to the future."
—JASON SCOTT, Archivist and owner of textfiles.com
(http://bkaprt.com/csm/58)

True confessions time: I'm intimidated by metadata. When the conversation at a cocktail party inevitably turns to metadata frameworks, semantic markup, and the pros and cons of various flavors of XML standards, my eyes start to wander over to the bar. And I've been a practicing information architect for more than fifteen years!

I don't tell you this to call into question my professional standing in the realm of library science. Instead, I want to reassure you: everyone, even people who live and breathe this stuff, can sometimes feel a bit out of their league when metadata comes up. I've discovered that people tend to glaze over when we talk about metadata, and that's unfortunate. More people—business owners, content creators, and production managers—need to wrap their heads around the benefits of having more and better metadata attached to their content.

I think people are put off because we tend to jump right into discussing how to create and deploy metadata before explaining *why*.

Why before how

Why should content creators have to enter content into separate fields in the CMS (or mark it up with semantic tags) even though that's not as easy or straightforward as simply entering it into a big blob? Because those fields and tags represent metadata—they provide more information about what the content is and how it can be used.

Why should content creators have to enter additional information about their content—expiration date, content priority, keywords, and tags—when they don't always know how that data will be used? Because having that information makes the content more flexible (and thus more valuable) in the future. Metadata is the foundation that allows you to achieve many of the other goals of adaptive content. If you're convinced that it's important to create reusable content, structured content, or presentation-independent content, then what that implies is you need to add more metadata:

- **Content reuse:** if you want your content to be able to live in many different places, if you want to target individual fields or content objects to different platforms, then you need metadata so each platform knows what to do.

- **Structured content:** when we talk about content models, content packages, and content chunks, we're really talking about metadata. When you define the fields your content will be chunked into, the labels attached to those fields, and the limits you assign to the data types that can be entered into those fields, you're defining the metadata that surrounds your content.

- **Presentation-independence:** think about all the cues we communicate through visual styling. We communicate the priority, hierarchy, and value of content to the reader by the weight and size of typography, or the layout and placement on the page. If we want truly platform-independent content, we can't rely on visual styling developed with a single platform in mind to retain this information. Instead, we need to develop ways to encode that meaning in our content—through metadata that tells us what the content means, not just how it should *look*.

And that's why we have content management technology.

Why we invented robots

Too often, people wind up fulfilling the technology's needs, as servants of their content management system, rather than having the tool support and facilitate their needs. We force people to conform to the system's needs as they fight their way through fields and dropdowns, rather than have the technology do what it does best: handle routine tasks automatically.

This is the whole reason we invented robots! Let's reclaim our right as humans to bend them to our will. As Rachel Lovinger explains (http://bkaprt.com/csm/50):

> *Content management tools that incorporate a wide range of structure and metadata capabilities will allow producers to create content that is more flexible, and encoded with meaningful metadata and semantic markup, without needing to understand all the underlying code. Content with "baked-in" semantic markup makes it faster, easier, and cheaper to bring new content products to market.*

Our content management tools should make it as easy as possible for humans to create structured, presentation-independent content that has the appropriate metadata so it can be flexibly reused. In fact, that's why the last attribute of adaptive content is having a **usable content management system.**

USABLE CMS

A good user experience in a CMS depends on having a well-defined authoring and publishing workflow:

- Technology is designed to facilitate user needs and goals, and users aren't expected to bend themselves to fit the system's requirements (this is user experience 101).
- Usability is evaluated on the overall workflow, not for individual screens. A particular form might be easy to fill out, but cumbersome when viewed in the context of the overall process.

- Organizations recognize that "content management" is bigger than just the CMS. The tool is there to facilitate and manage human processes and tasks, some of which by definition happen outside the system.

Fortunately, we have all kinds of techniques from the world of user experience design to help us create a more usable CMS. So whether you're researching new CMS products to implement an entirely new platform, or making changes to an existing CMS like WordPress or ExpressionEngine, you can evaluate and make changes to the CMS to provide a better user experience for your content authors.

CMS is the enterprise software that UX forgot

Many content management systems look like a database got drunk and vomited all over the interface (FIG 3.14).

Fields are scattered across the screen, with no rhyme or reason as to their placement. Field labels appear to have been assigned by a random word generator. Inconsistent labeling from screen to screen suggests they were assigned by someone with amnesia. Creating or editing a single piece of content forces content creators to bounce from screen to screen, a process requiring patience, attention to detail, and intestinal fortitude.

This is because, as Jeff Eaton of Lullabot explained to me, "Most CMSs were designed to provide an interface to a data model rather than to provide a user experience that helps content creators complete their tasks." In other words, the interface provides a window to the database fields, rather than a workflow designed to support user goals.

As a result, content creators complain about the CMS. They refuse to fill out more than the absolute bare minimum of fields, even though creating additional content chunks would make the content more flexible and more reusable. They demand a single blob of a field, into which they can dump anything they want—text, images, tables, Flash files—and then format and style them any way they want using a WYSIWYG toolbar.

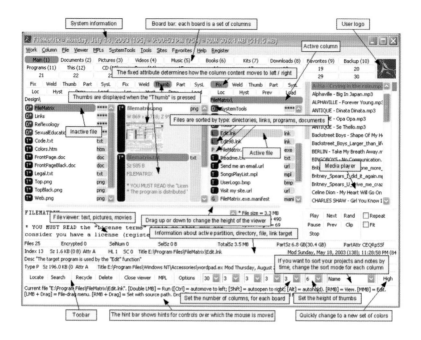

FIG 3.14: What? We wanted to make the workflow simpler so we put all the fields on one screen!

The solution here isn't to give in to their demands for a blob of text. The answer is that we need to improve the author experience in the CMS. The only way we're going to support future-friendly content management—a model that allows for flexible content reuse—is if we give content creators usable interfaces, workflows, and tools to make that happen.

Content modeling is the first step in this process. Rather than accepting the default content model baked into the CMS, designers and developers need to question its utility. What are all those fields? Do they need to be there? Are they in the right place? Are they sequenced appropriately on the screen? Are they labeled so they're meaningful to content authors?

For too long, we've abdicated responsibility for these choices to the CMS platform. If you're the designer or a developer who creates the website's authoring interface, then your job is to create a usable CMS. Don't just settle for the out-of-the-box interface—design a content authoring workflow that provides a good experience for your users.

Coupled vs. decoupled CMS

The problems with publishing content to mobile and other platforms go deep—way down to the depths of the server. If you want to deliver a great experience to mobile users, your CMS has to support it.

Bad news: your CMS probably doesn't support it. This is because your CMS is designed to publish to the desktop web. These systems are called "coupled CMSs." A coupled CMS doesn't allow you to tailor the experience for desktop vs. mobile users without significant custom development effort. If you're imagining an NPR-style COPE model, where you can model individual content objects and target them differently based on platform, you need a CMS that gives you a fine-grained level of control.

Most coupled CMSs don't have the capability to target content elements to different platforms based on a set of business rules. That's because, in a coupled CMS, the same monolithic system controls everything:

- Creating and editing content.
- Storing content in a defined data model.
- Displaying content in the presentation layer.
- Publishing and delivering the content to the user.

Decoupled CMSs (typically larger enterprise platforms) handle these tasks with independent systems. By decoupling content authoring from content display, we make multi-channel publishing possible.

Dan Willis, Director of Mobile Experience Design at Marriott explains: "Traditional publishing and content management systems bind content to display and delivery mechanisms, which forces a recycling approach for multi-platform publishing." Alternatively, in a decoupled system, "All display and workflow issues are addressed by delivery applications, rather than by a content management system earlier in the process," (http://bkaprt.com/csm/59).

If we want to deliver an experience optimized for a given platform (desktop, mobile web, app, television, what have you) then the decisions about how to display the content need to happen further downstream. If we want to be able to select which content chunks appear on a given platform, then we need a CMS that will support that.

Beware the preview button

Most content management tools have a "preview" button so the person who's editing content can see how it will look when it's published. It's one of the most requested features from content creators. When you click on that button, what does it show you?

Why, the desktop website, of course!

The fact that we can even offer a "preview" shows how tight the association is between content management and delivery. The content output is optimized for a particular display. There's no sense within the system that this content might be published to lots of different places. There's no way to show the content creators how their content might appear on a mobile website or in an app.

The existence of the preview button reinforces the notion that the desktop website is the "real" website and mobile is a satellite, an afterthought.

Showing a preview isn't inherently wrong—anyone who's ever printed out a letter for editing knows writers love to see their work in context. But from this point forward, assuming that a preview is merely the desktop website is wrong. Offering a true preview in the future will require that we find a way to help content creators envision their content in many different settings.

At this point in the history of mobile development, getting an accurate preview (or being able to do QA on different devices) is a challenging problem. Presumably in the future, there will be better ways to preview and do QA without having to buy dozens of different types of hardware. Most organizations can't afford to build a test lab with all the latest and greatest devices. Some local communities have stepped up to make shared device labs accessible to more people. Your organization might also allocate a budget for device purchases and try to find used ones. (More information about how to set up a device lab is available in the resources section at the back of the book.)

ADAPTIVE CONTENT FIRST

Adaptive content is a way to think beyond the platform. It puts your content at the center of your strategy and publishing process, right where it belongs. Instead of jumping right to worrying about the requirements and constraints of a particular platform or device, you're investing in the future of your content.

One of the most heated debates in mobile publishing is figuring out the relationship between the desktop content mothership, and all the different mobile platforms and devices. While publishing a small subset of content aimed at the "mobile use case" is the wrong strategy, does that mean organizations need to publish *exactly* the same content to the desktop and mobile? What happens if you need to structure content differently to accommodate different screen sizes and resolutions? How can you deal with content formats or sizes that simply won't work on mobile devices?

Adaptive content answers how to approach this problem. It's a path to *content parity*, where all users get a complete set of content—the exact same content when that's appropriate, and equivalent alternatives when it's not. Adaptive content gives you the flexibility to serve up different content *intentionally* to users, according to device, screen size, or context.

Adaptive content does this by creating well-structured, presentation-independent content. Content that was created from the start with the intent that it would be used in a variety of places. Content that includes the right metadata to help communicate what it means. And content that was published by a content management system that works the way users expect it to. Content that has a creation and maintenance workflow that reduces duplicate effort and makes the author's job easier.

One more thing: it was created with an adaptive content strategy process.

CONTENT STRATEGY FOR MOBILE: THE PROCESS

You want to be able to maintain a consistent base of content. You want to ensure you can communicate effectively in whichever channel your customer wants to consume your content. You might even need to stretch the same team and budget to do it.

So how do you make it happen? What needs to change? What stays the same about your current process, and in what ways will the way you work need to evolve?

In the following sections, we'll discuss the content strategy process with a focus on supporting multi-channel publishing. The next four sections will cover the big things you're going to need to do next:

1. First, you'll **define your strategy and put a plan in place** for how to get there. It's okay if you're not ready to jump in with both feet—but you do need to start planning now.
2. You'll **audit your content and edit where necessary.** Instead of imagining that you're writing for a single platform, you'll think about writing content so it can be reused. You may even create multiple versions for maximum reuse.
3. You'll **add more structure to your content.** Instead of writing pages of content, you'll develop an information architecture of content chunks that you can recombine in different ways.

4. You'll **change the way your people and processes work.**
You'll demand better tools and more streamlined, more effective workflows. And you'll have the right people working together in the right organizational structure to manage
your content across channels.

Ready to get started? Whether you're ready to dive right in
or just stick a toe in the water, you'll be better off if you put a
strategy in place first.

4

STRATEGY AND PLANNING

"LOFTY AMBITIONS," you might be thinking, "but it will take a long time to make this happen." If your organization is already challenged with maintaining and managing its web content, adding mobile into the mix can be daunting. The gap between where you are and where you want to be may feel insurmountable.

That's why we call it *strategy*.

This isn't about describing a vision for where you *should be* on mobile, and then feeling like a failure because you can't get there tomorrow. The goal is to clearly articulate where you want to be, and then take meaningful steps in that direction. The only way you'll get there is if you have a clear picture in mind of where you want to go.

But first, let's talk about what you can do starting *right now*.

BABY STEPS IN THE RIGHT DIRECTION

Maybe you're totally new to this whole mobile thing, and you're not sure where to start. Maybe you don't know enough about mobile to make good decisions about how to write, structure, and encode content. Maybe you understand it's important to deliver content on mobile, but the rest of your organization hasn't bought in yet.

Whatever is holding you back from developing your "official" content strategy for mobile shouldn't stop you from moving forward.

Gather analytics data

Many organizations have been spurred to develop a mobile website or app based on analysis of their log files and search analytics. If you're developing a mobile site for the first time, or looking to develop a more robust mobile experience that includes more content and features, looking at your analytics data will give you insights you can use to figure out how to proceed.

You might wish to gather data about the following, and evaluate whether it's time to make changes:

- Percentage of site visits that come from mobile browsers.
- Pages or sections of content being accessed on your desktop site from mobile browsers.
- Common search queries from mobile browsers.
- Search queries on mobile that get redirected to the mobile homepage, because the content doesn't exist on mobile.
- Exit pages where mobile users abandon your mobile site for the desktop site.

One caveat to keep in mind: many analytics packages are based on JavaScript, which isn't supported on many low-end mobile phones and older BlackBerry devices, which means the device doesn't get counted. Make sure you're getting an accurate picture of your audience by using an analytics approach (like server-side code snippets on Google Analytics) that actually counts *all* mobile users (http://bkaprt.com/csm/6o).

Conduct user research

Don't think your current mobile analytics and research on today's mobile websites will give you the whole picture. Today's crummy, crippled mobile experiences are inadequate environments to evaluate what people *really* want to do on mobile. To fully understand how people want to interact with your content on mobile, you must talk to them. If you've never done any user research or usability studies on how people interact with mobile devices, start now.

If your mobile site shows only a subset of content, and you're expecting your users to tap a full desktop website link to access your content, then the doctor calls for a usability test. See if people can actually find, read, and make decisions about content that requires them to pinch and zoom their way around a screen designed for a much larger monitor. Your findings may persuade you to invest in developing a full mobile site.

If you're ready to start putting together your mobile site or app, it's time to prototype and conduct iterative testing. There are many tools to help you develop quick mockups you can put in front of users. How else are you going to see your content in action?

Developing your mobile strategy will also take some imagination—which might come from looking at what other organizations are doing.

Conduct a competitive review

If you want to educate yourself and your team about the state of mobile content, there's no better way to see what's out there than by conducting a competitive review. Doing research on mobile sites or apps from competitors who are doing it right (or wrong) will help your team understand what works and what doesn't.

A word of warning: today's mobile experiences can be pretty lousy. Looking only at your competitors may not exactly inspire you to greatness. You'll also want to go outside your competitive set to look at best-in-class examples of mobile websites and apps, regardless of industry. Look for examples from publishers, retailers, and universities. Look especially at large-scale content sites, such as encyclopedias, how-to sites, medical and healthcare resources, and other reference guides.

Which devices to review

Given the state of the industry, it's likely that the primary form factor you'll want to review will be a smartphone, but it will be instructive to look at other devices as well. Some guidelines to help you prioritize which devices to review:

- If you're looking only at mobile websites, you can get away with reviewing either iPhone or Android but you don't need both. (This guidance applies because you'll be focused on the content, and not on features or interactions. If you were looking at interactive applications with lots of functionality, you might need to look at both.)
- If you're looking at mobile apps on smartphones then you should look at both iPhone and Android.
- Given the dominance of the Apple iPad in the tablet market, you should review content on this platform. One study reports that the iPad is responsible for 94.64 percent of all tablet web traffic (http://bkaprt.com/csm/61). Take special note of content that appears in apps optimized for the iPad; many of your competitors will likely rely on their desktop websites to support this form factor and may not have iPad-optimized mobile websites.
- If you have access to a Kindle Fire or Nexus 7, you should also look at content on a 7″ tablet, as this form factor is distinct from both smaller smartphones and larger tablets. As of February 2012 , the Kindle Fire had a 54.4 percent share of the Android market, making it the most popular Android tablet by a substantial margin (http://bkaprt.com/csm/62).
- Always cross-reference your review of the mobile sites and apps with the desktop site, so you can get a sense of how content is treated on each version.

How to evaluate

Develop a list of heuristics against which you'll evaluate each site. Potential dimensions on which you might evaluate competitors include:

- **Availability:** how many of your competitors even have a mobile website or app? If they do, are they offering a bare minimum of content and features, or do they go beyond that? What content and features do they offer, if they only show a subset?
- **Global navigation:** how do they handle global navigation? Does it include the same major categories as the desktop site, or just a subset? Are navigation categories prioritized differently for mobile? How does the user access the global navigation from the homepage and other site pages?
- **Wayfinding:** how easily can users get to their content destination? Do landing pages along the way offer meaningful navigation labels and useful teasers? Is the path to content quick and direct or does the user have to pogo-stick back and forth? How is section navigation presented in addition to global navigation?
- **Reading experience:** is the content easy to read on mobile? Is it written clearly? Is content that might appear on one page on the desktop split into multiple pages on mobile screens? If so, does that additional navigation make it easier or harder to read?
- **Content formatting:** is the content designed and formatted for mobile reading? Are content elements like tables, lists, and multi-column layouts appropriately transformed for a differently-sized screen?
- **Media:** how are large images or infographics treated? What about video or other interactive features?
- **Search:** is there a search function available on mobile devices? Do search results help or hinder the user in finding content? Can the user find content from an external search engine like Google, or does the search query just redirect to the mobile homepage?

Convince your CEO

Aim all your initial strategy and planning at one goal: convincing your CEO and executive team to invest more in content strategy for mobile (assuming they're not already on board). How you do that depends on your organization's personality. Consider the following:

- **Are they motivated by data?** Make sure you have analytics reports from your organization—and statistics from outside your company too. Mobile might seem small right now as a percentage of total traffic, but those numbers aren't going down. Demonstrate how mobile is poised to grow in the future.
- **Are they motivated by growth?** What company isn't? Focus on showing the size of the opportunity—and the opportunities that may be missed by not developing a strategy now.
- **Are they motivated by shame?** Teach them what makes a great experience on mobile, and how your organization isn't measuring up. In particular, if your competitor is doing things right, you'll likely be able to push all their buttons.
- **Are they motivated by usability?** (Lucky you.) Ask the executive team to give up their computers for a day or two and use only the mobile web. You might even direct them to try some common tasks using your website on mobile.

Don't forget: mobile is new to most people. Even seasoned digital executives can feel like neophytes when asked to make decisions about this new medium. Other executives often feel "digital fatigue" at the pace of change in our space. Part of your role is to help them feel comfortable and confident making decisions—don't make them feel like idiots who don't get it.

GIANT STEPS IN THE WRONG DIRECTION?

There's a difference between deciding to do something imperfectly in the short term, and believing that it's a good long-term solution. Design is often about making tradeoffs, and sometimes you make the wrong choices for the right reasons. As long as those decisions are conscious choices—made because of an immediate, short-term need to serve user expectations or meet business goals—there's nothing inherently wrong with taking a little detour on your way to the end goal. Just try not to get stuck at any of these way stations, okay?

Serve up a small subset of content and features

You might call this the "interim" mobile site. Or the "holy cats, we better get something up there quick!" mobile site. If looking at your analytics data and your competitive set makes you realize that you're way behind the curve, then by all means, don't delay. Build a mobile landing page today!

Remember the early days of the web, where "coming soon" pages were speckled through everyone's site navigation? Don't do that. You should especially avoid including animated GIFs of construction workers digging.

Instead, a dead-simple site, with the bare minimum of content and features, may suffice while you plan the rest of your mobile strategy. But do it with an eye to the future! This might be a good time to start your content inventory, and begin stakeholder discussions on how you'll evaluate your content. Perhaps you can start with an audit and analysis process in which you jointly discuss the merits of which content deserves to be included in the interim site. This exercise arms you for future prioritization exercises, and should give you a sense of whether reviewing and deleting content will go smoothly or painfully.

Fork your content

Yes, yes, the whole first section of this book was devoted to explaining why forking your content is a disaster. And now you find out it's okay!

It *can* be okay... as a temporary solution.

Developing a separate mobile experience—one that forks your content because it's not hooked up to your CMS—would be a maintenance nightmare in the long run. In the short-term, however, it may be the least bad option. If your mobile traffic is spiking and you realize you're losing business as a result, the cost of *not* developing a mobile website or app may be higher than the cost of building something with the intent of throwing it away.

But like a temporary dental crown or a spare automobile tire, don't expect to depend on your throwaway site forever. Building an interim site while you're working on a more robust solution is good! Forking your content and then thinking you've solved your mobile content strategy problem is bad. Got it?

Gerard Gober, Senior Director, Digital Experience at Comcast, explained to me in an interview why they developed a static mobile website to meet the immediate and growing demands users were making for content on mobile devices. They worked in parallel on a larger-scale solution that required changes to their CMS, knowing that they would replace the static site in the future:

We implemented a point solution knowing full well it was throwaway. In partnership with our leadership team, we had to make uncomfortable and difficult decisions that required quite a bit of courage. Ultimately, we're in business to add value for shareholders.

Design a responsive site that doesn't serve the desktop

Your future vision might include a single responsive website that will work across phones, tablets, and the desktop web. Designing and coding a responsive site might take a bit of time—even more time than it would take to develop a site for a single platform.

You know what might take even longer than that? Wrangling dozens of stakeholders to agree to make changes to the desktop site.

For better or for worse, within many organizations today, the desktop is still the "real" website, and mobile is a few people's hobby. The downside is that many still struggle to convince stakeholders and executives that investing in mobile is worth it. But the upside is that decisions about how to handle the mobile website aren't so fraught.

Organizations that want to provide an adaptive, sustainable solution for smartphone and tablet users—but who know that proposing a redesign of the desktop website will be a non-starter—might consider a responsive site for everything but the desktop. Who knows? The argument for extending the responsive design onto the desktop might come from users who say they prefer the cleaner, simpler, mobile experience.

Send people to the desktop site

Expecting mobile users to navigate your desktop site from their smartphone browser is not a long-term solution. It's not always a great experience for tablet users either, especially 7″ tablets. It's a total cop out to ask users to hunt around for the right content by pinching and zooming, and it's ergonomic lunacy to expect users to accurately hit tap targets sized for a 1024 pixel width screen. Just because we're used to it doesn't mean we should settle for it.

A link to the full desktop site on the mobile phone is acceptable only when it's the least bad option—if your choice is displaying the content formatted for the desktop, or not displaying the content at all, then use the desktop as a temporary fallback.

Keep in mind, however, that if you're delivering only a subset of your content optimized for mobile, and relying on a link to the full desktop website to show the remaining content, you're likely going to break search. If the search engine can see the content on the desktop site, but the content isn't available on the mobile site, the user gets unceremoniously dumped on the mobile homepage. Sure, that link to the desktop site is available, but you're forcing the user to start from the desktop homepage and swim around in your site navigation, trying to find content she should be able to access with one click from the search results. So don't redirect searches to your mobile site unless you provide *all* your content on mobile.

Short-term tactics, long-term planning

Just because you know you're building a temporary solution doesn't mean it can't have value for your long-term plans too. It may be that prioritizing and filtering your content for an "interim" site will help you plan for and focus on what you need to do for your "real" mobile content. Or it may be that the decisions you make for a responsive mobile version eventually carry over to the desktop site.

The way you get the most value from a short-term solution —even one that you know you're going to throw away—is if you have articulated your overall content strategy and you know where you're headed. That way, even if what you're doing in the immediate term isn't the ideal, you can plan to make it a stepping stone along the way.

Gerard Gober of Comcast explains:

> The biggest thing is, you have to have a content strategy in place. You have to know the end state you want.

THE DESIRED STATE

If you're ready to start developing your content strategy for mobile, then your first job is to define where you want to go.

I like to call this "putting a flag in the sand." As you move forward in the months and years to come, you'll have many decisions to make that will affect your mobile strategy and your content strategy. If your team can see the flag in the sand—even if it's way off in the distance—they'll at least know if their choices are moving them closer to or further away from the flag.

Your desired end state will be unique to your organization, but it might look something like the following:

- All of your content is available to users regardless of the platform they want to consume it on. You've achieved content parity: you provide the same content where it's feasible, and equivalent content where it's not.

- Your content is well-written and it all provides value to your reader. Mobile might provide a useful lens for doing the audit and analysis, but your goal isn't just better content for the mobile site. Instead, you have a process in place to evaluate and remove content that's not working—wherever it might appear.
- Your content is written and structured for maximum reuse. You've identified a system of reusable text elements written for reading and navigation. You've also figured out how your images, tables, charts, videos, etc., will scale across different device resolutions.
- Your content management system has been tweaked—or completely overhauled—to support multi-channel publishing. You've got a tool that provides a good user experience for your content authors, and supports them in developing the content structures needed. If you need to prioritize your content differently for mobile, or serve up alternative content for elements that won't work on mobile, your CMS is technically robust enough to allow you to target content according to metadata and business rules.
- You've put a plan in place for doing qualitative and quantitative research to help you understand how people are using your mobile content, and how that might differ from the desktop. You're analyzing data provided by your analytics package and search queries, and using it to make informed choices about how to prioritize. When there are questions you can't answer just by looking at data, you talk to actual people.
- You recognize that a successful content strategy for mobile comes from deep inside. You have internal processes and an editorial workflow in place to make sure that your content is updated when necessary, evaluated regularly to make sure it's doing its job, and retired when its time is up. You have an organizational structure and incentive system that supports—even rewards—people for working together to develop an integrated and holistic approach to content across channels.

Sound like content paradise? A totally unrealistic, *Fantasy Island* content nirvana? It's not an unattainable dream. In the upcoming sections of this book, we'll talk through each of these in more detail, describing what you need to do to get there.

WHAT'S NEXT

We've discussed how to start planning your content strategy for mobile—even if you're just getting started and need to take baby steps. If you're ready to plant your flag and start off on the path to creating better mobile content, here's what's in store for you next:

- **Writing and editing:** your mobile content strategy can be a catalyst to help you improve the quality of all your content.
- **Information architecture:** you don't want to publish totally different content to mobile, but you may need to structure it or prioritize it differently. We'll talk about how to make that happen without wasted effort.
- **People and process:** successful multi-channel publishing will require changes to the way you work. We'll discuss how your leadership and workflow will need to evolve.

Let's take a look at how mobile can help you pare down your content and write more effectively—wherever your content might appear.

5 WRITING AND EDITING

ARE WE REALLY going to talk about writing content for mobile, after we've spent so much time explaining how you can't create content for a single platform? Here's a neat trick: we're going to use mobile as a lens to make all our content better, regardless of platform.

There is no "how to write for mobile." There's only good writing. Period.

That said, mobile gives us an opportunity to review our content within some tight constraints. Imagining how we're going to take the vast expanses of content we've created for the desktop web (and in print) and squish it onto tiny screens will help us prioritize. Realizing that some of the dreck on our desktop sites doesn't deserve to be on the mobile site will inspire us to edit it down—or remove it entirely.

How are we going to make this magic happen? We're going to dip into our trusty bag of content strategy tricks, and follow the same processes and activities using the same tools and deliverables as we would for, say, a web content strategy project.

But this time, we're going to imagine that we're doing them with the intent to put content onto a mobile website or app. "But isn't the whole point to get our content ready to go *anywhere?*" you might wonder? It is. Mobile is the catalyst that will help people get there. So use it as a tool. Feel free to get your content owners and business stakeholders thinking about the challenges of the smartphone form factor. If necessary, the fact that you're using these exercises to improve *all* your content can be our little secret.

CONTENT INVENTORY AND AUDIT

"If it shouldn't be on the mobile site, it shouldn't be on the desktop site either!"

This rallying cry for "mobile first" offers a glimpse of a fit and friendly future, one where content owners and stakeholders all agree to cut the fat out of a desktop website that's grown too big for its pants. Once they imagine their bloated content squeezed onto a tiny screen, they'll be motivated to trim it down.

Like any diet, it's easier said than done.

Kristina Halvorson, CEO of Brain Traffic, is fond of pointing out that there is no "magical database in the sky" that will spit out the content for your website. I'm here to tell you that there is also no magical liposuction machine in the sky that will reach down and vacuum out your flabby content.

You're going to have to do it yourself, the old-fashioned way: with a giant spreadsheet.

The basic tools for analyzing what you've got are the content inventory and the content audit—these don't change just because you're thinking about mobile. Looking at your content through the lens of mobile does provide some helpful perspective when you're documenting the inventory and conducting the audit.

Inventory

When you take a content inventory, you take an objective look at the content assets you have to work with. Typically,

Section		Page Name	Page Template	URL	Owner	Last Update	Keywords	Page Rank	Notes
0.0	Home	Homepage	Homepage			4/17/2012			
1.0	Our Products	Our Products Landing Page	Landing page			6/18/2011			
1.1	Our Products	Acme Cage Mousetrap	Product page			6/18/2011			All product pages contain description, image and specs
1.2	Our Products	Acme Snap Mousetrap	Product page			6/18/2011			
1.3	Our Products	Acme Glue Mousetrap	Product page			6/18/2011			
1.4	Our Products	Acme Mouse Poison	Product page			6/18/2011			
1.5	Our Products	Acme Live-Catch Mousetrap	Product page			6/18/2011			
1.6	Our Products	Acme Bucket Trap	Product page			6/18/2011			
2.0	Our Services	Our Services Landing Page	Landing page						
2.1	Our Services	In-home Consultation	Landing page						
2.2.0	Our Services	Rodent Control Services	Landing page						
2.2.1	Our Services	Trap Setting and Removal	Article Page						
2.2.2	Our Services	Rodenticide Sprays	Article Page						
2.2.3	Our Services	Mouse Contraceptives	Article Page						
2.2.4	Our Services	Varmint Hunting	Article Page						
2.2.5	Our Services	Cat Rental	Article Page						
2.3	Our Services	Request a Brochure	Form						Sends to Excel

FIG 5.1: In a standard content inventory, determine which data you want to gather about your content and assign those categories to columns in your spreadsheet.

people conduct these when they're redesigning a website and need to understand the size and scope of the project. You can follow a similar process when you think about getting your content ready to be displayed on a variety of mobile screens.

A content inventory is a quantitative assessment of your content. You're not trying to judge the quality of the content yet (that comes later, in the content audit). You're just trying to get your arms around what you've got.

Standard inventory categories

In preparing a content inventory, you might expect to gather some of the following facts about your content. Think of these as the columns in your spreadsheet (FIG 5.1):

- Unique ID number or code for each line in your inventory (numbers map to pages).
- Site section, or where it sits in the site hierarchy.
- Page title, including the main title and what appears in the meta <title> tag.
- Page URL.
- Content owner and/or person who last updated the page.
- Date the page was created and/or last updated.
- Expiration date assigned to the page, if any.

- Keywords that describe the page, or keywords used to index the page for search.
- Page rank or number of visits.
- Date the page was last visited, especially noting pages with no visits within a period of time (say, six months or one year).
- Content type or the CMS template used.

Because content inventories gather quantitative, objective data, it's tempting to want to use an automated tool to crawl the site. Isn't robotic work like this the thing machines are best at? Certainly, some of this data can be pulled directly from the CMS or gathered using a crawler, but there's real value in the editorial insight you gain in systematically reviewing the pages, so think of automation as a supplement to human effort, rather than a replacement for it. (In general that mindset is what will protect us from our robot overlords.)

Mobile inventory categories

When you're inventorying your content for a future life on mobile screens, there are other objective data you can gather.

Since getting content onto different screen sizes and resolutions will often require breaking it into smaller chunks than the desktop page, you need to have an approach to inventorying that tracks individual chunks or modules, not just pages. You might think of these as rows in an outline table (FIG 5.2):

- Unique ID number or code for each content chunk in your inventory (letters map to chunks within pages).
- Character or word count for headlines, subheads, and page summaries.
- Character or word count for body copy.
- Image dimensions or standard crop ratios or cut sizes—especially note large infographics or other dense images that won't scale well to smaller screens.
- Content styling, especially in columns, tables, or lists, that may need to be presented differently on smaller screens.

	Section	Page/Object Name	Template/Content Type	URL	Owner	Last Update	Keywords	Size	Page Rank	Notes
	0.0	Home	Homepage	Homepage			4/17/2012				
	1.0	Our Products	Our Products Landing Page	Landing page			6/18/2011				
	1.0.a		Headings	Text					6@100 char		
	1.0.b		Body copy	Text					6@500 words		
	1.0.c		Images	PNG					6@300x250		
	1.0.d		Infographic	Flash							
	1.1	Our Products	Acme Cage Mousetrap	Product page			6/18/2011				All product pa contain descri image and spe
	1.2	Our Products	Acme Snap Mousetrap	Product page			6/18/2011				
	1.3	Our Products	Acme Glue Mousetrap	Product page			6/18/2011				
	1.4	Our Products	Acme Mouse Poison	Product page			6/18/2011				
	1.5	Our Products	Acme Live-Catch Mousetrap	Product page			6/18/2011				
	1.6	Our Products	Acme Bucket Trap	Product page			6/18/2011				
	2.0	Our Services	Our Services Landing Page	Landing page							
	2.1	Our Services	In-home Consultation	Landing page							
	2.2.0	Our Services	Rodent Control Services	Landing page							
	2.2.1	Our Services	Trap Setting and Removal	Article Page							
	2.2.2	Our Services	Rodenticide Sprays	Article Page							
	2.2.3	Our Services	Mouse Contraceptives	Article Page							
	2.2.4	Our Services	Varmint Hunting	Article Page							
	2.2.5	Our Services	Cat Rental	Article Page							
	2.3	Our Services	Request a Brochure	Form							Sends to Exce
	3.0	News and Insights	News and Insights Landing Page	Editorially controlled page			4/17/2012				
	3.1.0	News and Insights	Pest Control Perspectives	Listing Page			4/17/2012				
	3.1.1	News and Insights	New Developments in Possum Monitoring	Individual Whitepaper			4/1/2012				
	3.1.1.a			PDF							
	3.1.2	News and Insights	Improving Pest Management and Reducing Pesticide Risks in Schools and Parks	Individual Whitepaper			3/1/2012				
	3.1.3	News and Insights	Is Pest Control for the	Individual Whitepaper			2/1/2012				

FIG 5.2: Because content inventories for mobile need to look at a finer grain of detail, you may need a more complex spreadsheet. One option is to use the Outline Table function in Excel to add sub-rows.

- Content format, especially .pdf, .doc, .ppt, or other document formats that won't condense well on smaller screens.
- Content presented using Flash or any other technology that just won't work on some mobile devices.
- Common modules reused across pages (for example, in the right column) which you may need to handle differently on smaller screens or even eliminate on less capable devices.
- Content chunks that may be stored in different database locations, which may affect how easily you can repurpose them (for example, user comments are often stored in a different database from managed content).

Inventorying at this level is something most automated systems aren't set up to do easily. Make friends with your tech team—they're the ones who can help you figure out things like character counts and database locations.

Representative sampling

If you're freaking out because your website is simply too big to inventory, don't despair. Just like it wouldn't be possible to survey every single person in your country, you don't always need to look at every single page in your site. Instead, you can take a *representative sample* of pages.

When inventorying, it's most important to set up your approach to how you'll tackle the problem. Before diving into your full inventory, do a quick pass through the site to determine:

- **Breadth of your audit:** do you need to look at every section, or will it be sufficient to focus on a single section?
- **Depth of your audit:** do you need to dig into every level of the site, or can you stop at a certain point, say four or five levels down?
- **Range of content types:** it's less important that you see every unique page, and more important that you understand the different content types—a quick review can give you a sense of whether you're dealing with many consistent pages (like article pages or product pages with a regular structure) or lots of one-offs.

Remember, your inventory isn't a document you complete once and then stick on a shelf to gather dust. You can and should keep adding to it as you go through this process.

Audit

By now, you understand that you're not trying to create a totally separate mobile website, with a unique subset of content—right? Keeping in mind that your goal is to apply any improvements to *all* your content, you can still conduct this audit with mobile in mind.

You might imagine, then, that you're trying to decide whether each piece of content is worthy of being migrated to a new mobile website. What if your stakeholders and content owners had to physically move each piece of content to its new home? Would it merit the effort?

Audit criteria

To conduct your audit, you may wish to evaluate your content against criteria like the following:

- Subjectively, is each page or content chunk too long, too short, or just right? Length isn't inherently a problem, but you're trying to assess whether you can easily break longer pages into shorter chunks, or whether it makes sense to keep the whole document together.
- Is the text wordy or does it ramble? Is the language filled with jargon or marketing-speak? If you imagine a smaller screen, could you edit the text and clean up the wording without losing any meaning or value?
- Does each page or content chunk get to the point? Are the main ideas presented quickly and succinctly—in the first paragraph or in the page summary? If you imagine a user glancing at a mobile screen, would she get the main message right away?
- Is the content structured into chunks say, broken up with headings, or with teaser-sized chunks on landing pages? Does each chunk or paragraph present one and only one topic?
- Is the content up-to-date? Would anyone say "we don't need to put that content on the mobile website, it's too old"?
- Is the content useful and important? Would your stakeholders say that each page or content chunk is a must-have or a nice-to-have on mobile?

ANALYSIS

The point of doing an inventory and an audit isn't to create documentation—it's to drive change within your organization. Once you've taken a deep dive into your content, you need to communicate your findings and recommendations to your stakeholders and get them to agree on next steps. A gap analysis can help you figure out how to get from where you are to where you want to be.

Gap analysis

By the time you're done with your audit, you should have quite a bit of data to help inform your decisions about what to do with your content next. Based on your audit criteria, you have some decisions to make.

Your job, then, is to use mobile as a filter, to persuade your stakeholders and subject matter experts to act on each and every piece of content. Those actions will be:

- **Keep** it as-is and include it on the mobile website.
- **Revise** and edit to tighten up the writing or to create a more mobile-friendly format.
- **Delete** it, because it's irrelevant, not useful, or outdated.
- **Create new** content, perhaps to take advantage of new capabilities on mobile devices.

You'll probably want to add a new set of columns to your spreadsheet—or even a new sheet to your workbook—to help you track all the decisions you've made and actions you need to take next.

Communicating findings and recommendations

Mobile isn't magic. Simply waving a smartphone in a stakeholder's face and pointing to the smaller screen size won't necessarily help you convince him that his precious content isn't worthy of appearing on your mobile website. As with any evaluation process, the art of the content audit is the art of persuasion.

Education

Many of your stakeholders will be unfamiliar with mobile best practices—even people who are intimately familiar with making decisions about how the desktop web should function. As a result, you may encounter resistance and knee-jerk reactions, which are usually rooted in fear of not understanding how and why mobile is different. Use lots of best practice examples from other mobile websites and apps to make your point.

Content recommendations

Your job in presenting your content audit is to convince your stakeholders that the content needs to change. Think about which formats will be most persuasive to them. Some organizations value quantitative decision making. If that's your company, then score all your content on a rating scale, and show them charts and graphs to illustrate your main points. Other companies will be persuaded if you show them usability evaluations, competitive reviews, or even your expert opinion. Tailor your approach to how you present your recommendations so it's aligned with how people make decisions.

Desktop first!

Some of your constituents may still be imagining that you're planning to create a mobile website that contains less or different content than the desktop. By using mobile as a way to force them to filter, you may have allowed them to keep believing that the desktop is going to stay the same. Now, you'll need to get them on board with making edits to the content across the board. Emphasize the benefits of simplifying content for all users, and the pain of having to maintain multiple versions—enlist the CMS in your argument and explain that it prefers to serve one set of content.

EDITING

Imagine all you had was a mobile app or mobile website. No vast expanses of desktop screen real estate. No way to present every possible option on the screen at the same time, assuming that the user would figure it out. No presumption that your reader was sitting, transfixed, poring over every word.

With the limitations of a mobile screen as a guideline and a barrier, you'd naturally have to write differently. You'd get to the point. You'd put the most important information up front. You'd remove all the marketing jargon and fluff. You'd write short, declarative sentences. You wouldn't use a long word when a short one would do. You'd make every word earn its place.

Writing this way isn't just good writing for mobile. It's good writing for everyone. Here's how to use mobile to help edit your content.

Messaging

People have always tended to scan, rather than read, on the web. Desktop users skim their way through the text, alighting on headings and links and bullet points, searching for the information that matters to them.

Unless you're completely focused on what you want to communicate, you can't assume that your reader will get the message. Successful web writers know that they may only have a few seconds, a glance at the screen, to get the key idea across. Once they've grabbed the reader with a message that resonates, they might earn a bit more attention—but they can't squander it. Additional information needs to answer the user's follow-up questions and reinforce the main idea.

What was true on the web is even more true on mobile. It's not that people *won't* read on their mobile devices—it's that you have to earn their attention more than ever.

The limits of mobile provide a useful focusing device. When revising your content, use the constraints of a mobile screen as a guideline to help you hone your message and make sure it gets through (**FIG 5.3**):

· **Primary message:** what's the main idea you need to get across? Figure out what that is, and make sure readers can apprehend it in a glance at the screen. This primary message may come through in the headline, the summary, or the text's first sentence or two. Ideally, the primary message for any given page reinforces your overall brand and mission.

FIG 5.3: Use the mobile screen's constraints to help prioritize your primary message, secondary message, and supporting messages.

- **Secondary message:** assuming you've got their attention, what do you want them to know next? Once you've piqued your reader's interest, you can assume she'll be willing to read a bit more—maybe ten seconds or so, which is about the amount of time it would take to read the text on a standard mobile phone screen. (Assume a standard screen will fit approximately 100 words, give or take, depending on the design.) Answer her key questions: what is this, and why should I care? Remember, they're still likely to scan the screen looking for keywords that meet their goals.
- **Supporting messages:** what's next? What else do they need to know? Perhaps these points take the user to supplementary pages, or present related ideas in a list of bullet points. The key here (as always) is they're concise, loaded with words the user is scanning for, and make the user feel confident in her next tap.

Revisions

Here's a summary of guidelines to use when you revise your content for mobile. Just remember: these recommendations apply regardless of platform or channel. Mobile is just a useful constraint:

- **Plain language:** use shorter, simpler words. Write short sentences and avoid convoluted sentence structure.
- **Objective language:** neutral language is easier to read and more credible than marketing fluff. Use words your user will know, not jargon.
- **Be concise:** aim to get your main point across on a single screen, which is approximately 100 words. Ruthlessly delete unnecessary words. (That doesn't mean all anyone will read is a single screen—but it provides a helpful editing guideline.)
- **Write headings as links:** assume that headings and subheads could be repurposed as navigation. Make them actionable and fill them with trigger words—words that users themselves would say if asked to describe what they're looking for.
- **Write the first sentence as a summary:** assume that the first line of the page or section could be repurposed as a navigation summary. Put the main idea and important keywords in the first sentence.
- **Inverted pyramid:** don't bury the lede. Start with the conclusion. Put the most important ideas first. Bottom line up front (BLUF).
- **One topic per paragraph:** when readers scan the page, they look at initial sentences for main ideas. If additional ideas are presented in a single paragraph, users are likely to skip over them.
- **Highlight keywords:** readers scan for hyperlinks in text, so this is a particularly effective way to highlight. You may also bold keywords, but avoid color variations or underlining words that aren't hyperlinks.

Understanding Your Bill

Updated 3/9/2012 8:46:02 PM by Comcast Expert

✉ Email 🖨 Print   f Like   f Send   🐦 Tweet

Here's an overview of everything that will appear on your bill, so you can feel comfortable that you know what you're paying for and what to expect each month. We'll also go over specific information about what to expect on your first bill.

There are certain things you'll always see on your bill and certain things that you'll only see when adding new products or services or making remaining payments on a deferred payment plan.

FIG 5.4: Comcast edited the page that helps you understand your bill, making it easier to read without losing the meaning.

- **Bulleted lists:** use bullet points to make supporting ideas easy to scan.

Take your cues from Comcast. They edited and simplified the page that explains your bill, reducing the length and complexity of the language without losing any of the meaning (FIG 5.4).

COMING UP

By now, you should have a plan for how to move forward with your content strategy—or at least, be headed in the right direction.

You'll also have inventoried, audited, and analyzed your content so you know what needs to change. You've edited your content—or removed it entirely—so it provides maximum value.

Now, it's time to look at how your content is structured. What specific changes do you need to make to the way you architect your content to support multi-channel publishing?

After that, we'll look at what needs to change in your internal organization. How will your people and your processes need to adapt to adaptive content?

6 INFORMATION ARCHITECTURE

PRINT IS SO EASY, RIGHT? You put the ink on the paper and you know it will stay there. You don't have to worry about updating it all the time. Want to make changes, or release a new version? Better chop down some more trees. That'll take some time, so you'll have a chance to think carefully about your revisions.

Your iPad app isn't print. Neither is your mobile website, your Android app, or any other mobile "version" you might want to publish. Neither is your desktop website. Digital content is dynamic, flexible, fluid, and always updated.

Sound obvious? Unfortunately, we're still trying to get there.

The legacy of print is still with us on the web. We've moved from imagining how our content will look and where it will live in a printed document to imagining how it will look and where it will live on a webpage. We treat the desktop web like a dynamic document—sure, we have the flexibility to update it whenever we want, but it's still the one and only place our content will ever "live."

Those days are over.

How do we take what we know about information architecture and navigation design for mouse pointers, and adapt and evolve those models so they will also work for meat pointers? If we recognize we have to create new, flexible structures in our content, how do we do that? If we want to stop thinking about "pages" and start thinking about "packages," how does our editorial process need to change?

We've got work to do. Let's look at some key content structures and talk about what needs to evolve.

WAYFINDING

The web is all about action verbs. We click. We search. We navigate. We select. On every screen, we present users with options and ask them to take an action. Successful content puts the user in the driver's seat, helping guide them to where they want to go.

Jared Spool, CEO and Founding Principal of User Interface Engineering, often writes and speaks about the "scent of information" and how to write links using "trigger words"—words that inspire users to act because they make it obvious what will happen when users click on them. He says, "It shouldn't be news or a surprise to anyone in the world of website usability that having clear links that describe what the user will find after clicking is a priority in the design process" (http://bkaprt.com/csm/63).

What's true for the desktop web is even more important when users navigate your content on mobile. Smaller screen sizes mean that the user may have to drill down further to get to the content. Slower connections (paid for by the megabyte) mean the cost-per-tap may be higher. And because users just aren't as familiar with navigating on mobile, it will be easier for them to get lost. All the more reason to make sure that your wayfinding content—labels, summaries, and other microcopy—helps the user feel confident she's on the right track.

Don't rely on navigation labels alone

Tap. Refresh. Scan. Back. Tap. Refresh. Scan. Back.

How many times do you think your mobile user will do that before getting frustrated and give up?

If you're still imagining the mobile use case—the pressed for time, on-the-go, distracted mobile user—you're not going to make that user's life easier simply by putting location-based services on the home screen. Serving the mobile user means ensuring that she has enough context to quickly and easily find what she's looking for, even if it's several levels deep in the site. (Sounds a lot like what it means to deliver a good experience for the desktop user, doesn't it?)

A couple of taps off the main screen is when most mobile experiences start to break down. The architecture and design attention that gets lavished on the homepage and the main navigation bar doesn't make it to some of the more pedestrian screens, the way stations along the route to the content. Instead, users get a long list of links, many of which don't make much sense. How do they know which one to tap (**FIG 6.1**)?

Do provide a short teaser

"In its purest format, progressive disclosure is about offering a good teaser."
—**FRANK SPILLERS** (http://bkaprt.com/csm/64)

Progressive disclosure orients users in steps or stages that reveal more complex information as they go, helping them make good choices as they complete a task or navigate information. It's an old concept in human-computer interaction, first applied to early software interfaces in the 1980s. Its usefulness has been proven again and again on web-based interfaces, and it's easy to see how it applies to the constraints of smaller mobile devices.

Writing a good teaser is one of the simplest things you can do to help your users orient themselves so they can find

FIG 6.1: Verizon presumably knows the difference between its "Backup Assistant," "Backup Assistant Plus," and "Backup AssistantSM." Users won't. A short teaser would provide more context.

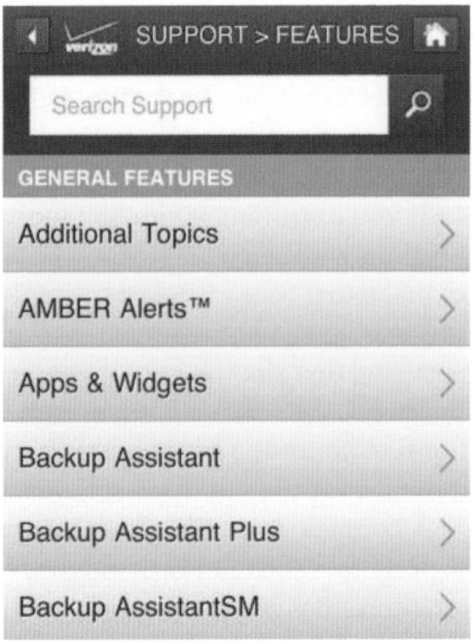

FIG 6.2: Comcast writes a short teaser for each navigation option. Even a single sentence can help users decide if they're in the right place and whether it's worth it to keep tapping.

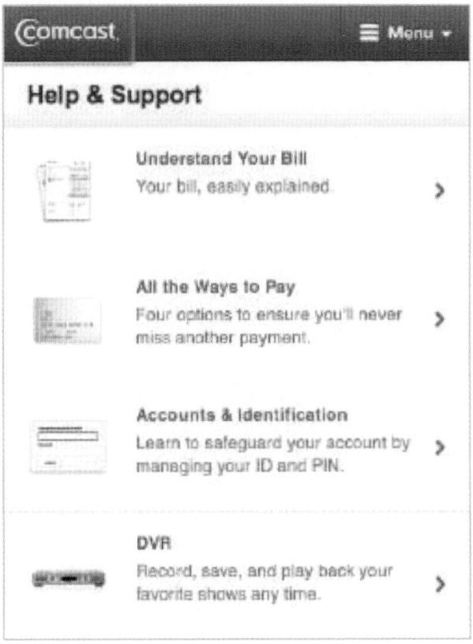

what they're looking for. Unfortunately, it's often one of the most overlooked. Write a sentence or two that describes each link. Fill that description with trigger words—words that users themselves would say if asked to describe what they're looking for (**FIG 6.2**). You'll ensure that each tap adds value, and reduce the risk that users will ping-pong back and forth between screens.

Truncation is not a content strate...

Where are all those teasers going to come from? If they don't exist already, then you're going to have to write them (and make sure there's a home for them inside your CMS). Don't fall into the trap of thinking that you can simply display the first sentence or two of your body copy, then drop in an ellipsis.

Unless you intentionally wrote the text to be a great teaser, it probably won't be. Crafting a teaser is an art—and it's different from writing the first sentence or two of your content.

Amazon does an admirable job of making their vast product catalog accessible on mobile devices, and they gain significant business value by enabling shoppers to purchase from their smartphones. But they miss the mark in presenting navigation teasers that entice users to take action. Why? They're recycling content from the desktop site and truncating it for summaries (**FIG 6.3**).

Not written for reuse

Taking text intended for use on the desktop site means you don't know what you'll get when it appears on a smaller mobile screen. Information like the name of the product is duplicated over and over, wasting space and providing little value to the user.

No trigger words

The whole point of writing a teaser is to stuff it full of the words your readers are thinking of when they describe what they're looking for. The first sentence or two of Amazon's

Product Description
Color: Red

From the Manufacturer

Make memories and share joy with Nikon's new high-resolution Coolpix L22 and its 12.0 effective megapixels, 3.6x zoom and huge, bright 3.0-inch LCD. Nikon's 3-way VR Image Stabilization System automatically detects subject movement and adjusts the shutter speed and ISO to compensate for camera shake and minimize image blur. The camera's Easy Auto Mode with Scene Auto Selector simplifies your picture-taking experience by letting camera automatically select the best setting to get great pictures. Nikon's Smart Portrait System will; fix red-eye, detect faces, fire the shutter when your subject smiles and warn you if they blink, to get you great portraits.

Carefree operation and high performance combined for consistently great pictures

Combining the precision optics of a Nikkor lens with the image quality and performance benefits of Nikon's innovative EXPEED digital image-processing concept, the Coolpix L22 is a quality compact digital camera that combines high performance with outstanding operating ease.

Intuitive and automated operation ensures carefree command over the high performance features of the Coolpix L22. Activated in Easy Auto Mode, Nikon's Scene Auto Selector makes capturing special moments as easy as turning on the camera and shooting without worrying about any settings. Electronic VR image stabilization, Motion Detection, Nikon's BSS (Best Shot Selector) function and ISO 1600 capability help ensure sharper results in lower light, or when capturing fast-moving subjects.

The Coolpix L22 is powered by AA size/R6 batteries, for the added advantage of being able to pick up a new set in virtually any corner of the world. The Coolpix L22 provides reassuring freedom from any worries about recharging or running out of power when a special shutter chance presents itself.

The large high-resolution 3-inch LCD monitor offers a bright image that is a pleasure to view, even outdoors. Controls are sized and placed to ensure intuitive operation. For example, dedicated buttons on the back of the body make it easy to switch between shooting and playback modes. And the contours of the large thumb rest and the body itself assure a solid grip. Design is just one aspect of the Coolpix L22 that combines beauty and functionality.

Nikon Coolpix L22 Feature Highlights

EXPEED digital imaging technology
Nikon's smarter approach to digital imaging technology. From image capture to processing, Nikon's comprehensive EXPEED digital imaging concept encompasses the entire picture-taking operation. EXPEED is much more than a processing engine; it is a revolution in digital photography.

Intelligent automation contributes to carefree shooting
Easy Auto Mode simplifies photography by taking control of settings; just turn on the camera and shoot freely. Activated in Easy Auto Mode, Nikon's Scene Auto Selector eliminates the need to manually select a scene mode to match the shot, making it faster and easier to capture the moment in beautiful fashion. The Coolpix L22 and L21 use this intelligent function to analyze the subject and its surrounding settings and automatically select the most appropriate scene mode to achieve optimal results.

FIG 6.3: Copy that makes sense in the context of Amazon's desktop product page makes for a lousy teaser. It lacks seductive trigger words, valuable space is wasted repeating the product name, and a bulleted list is just plain wrong for this context.

Nikon Coolpix...   **Details & Features**

Nikon Coolpix L22 12.0MP Digital Camera with 3.6x Optical Zoom and 3.0-Inch LCD (Red-primary)
Nikon
$102.29 + $5.49 Shipping

Product Features
· 12.0 megapixels for stunning prints as large as 16 x 20 inches   · 3.6x Zoom-NIKKOR glass lens (37mm to 134mm);...   >

From the Manufacturer
Make memories and share joy with Nikon's new high-resolution Coolpix L22 and its 12.0 effective megapixels, 3.6x zoom and...   >

Product Description
Nikon Coolpix L22 12MP Digital Camera (Red)   >

Home   Search   Cart   Wish List   More

body copy wasn't written with that goal in mind, which means that instead of tightly written navigation copy designed to get users to tap, they present fluffy marketing copy that doesn't communicate anything.

Not formatted appropriately

Amazon has all kinds of formatting lurking in its big blob of body copy. The bulleted list shown here was never intended to be taken out of context and crammed into a tiny tap target. Same goes for subheadings, pull quotes, tables, and other formatted text.

PAGE TITLES AND HEADLINES

What's in a page title? Would a page by any other name be just as findable?

Whether it's a product page, an article, a blog post, or a support topic, what you call your page is crucial to helping users find it.

Page titles don't just appear at the top of the page. Headlines also appear in links that help users find that page. So, your page titles and headlines will now pop up in more and more places: links on homepages and landing pages (both desktop and mobile), lists of links in sidebars and other related content, search results (both internal and external), in social media like Twitter and Facebook, and, yes, in their rightful place at the top of the screen. Given all these variables for how and where page headings might appear, it's helpful to think of them as a system.

Don't truncate headlines

This should go without saying, right? Just because you can't count on having a large screen size or high resolution display doesn't give you license to chop off page titles or headlines wherever you feel like it. *The Daily Beast* commits a litany of abuses on their mobile site—truncating headlines (presumably because there isn't enough space?) and then wasting space

FIG 6.4: Apparently *The Daily Beast* needed to save space so they could include a byline and then repeat the author's name in the summary.

by repeating the author's byline in two places (**FIG 6.4**). Space may be at a premium, but use it wisely.

But what if the constraints of your device context or screen real estate mean that your headline won't fit? You will need to create multiple versions of headlines to support all these different uses. Before you freak out about all the extra work implied by that, take a step back and think about how to create a system of headlines.

Do write a system of headlines

I get to look a lot of companies' content management underpants. Peeking inside a CMS, I often find writers asked to create some combination of the following:

- Article headline
- Teaser headline
- Homepage headline
- Landing page headline
- External SEO headline
- Internal search headline
- Facebook headline
- Twitter headline
- iPhone headline
- Android headline

Can I get a chorus here? *Don't create content for a specific context.* Sing it!

Instead, tell your writers to focus on writing a few headline types, and then have each platform show the one that best fits its constraints. By devising a system of headlines that will cover a range of possible options, you can publish the right headlines and page titles to all these different contexts, without truncating the text.

This all comes back to your content management system. You need a tool that encourages your writers to create just the right number of headlines—so that the right headlines can be served up to each platform, as needed.

For starters, consider two major variables:

Length

For Twitter, the most extreme example, you have only 60-100 characters to work with, since you will also include a link to your website and potentially cite a source. A headline that's short enough for Twitter could work well in mobile contexts too.

You might just write one short headline and use it everywhere, but why limit the capabilities of platforms that can show more? You can use longer versions (100-200 characters) to provide more information in platforms that can support it.

Tone and style

Who are you writing your headlines for: people or robots? Of course, you want to write a headline that's meaningful—even delightful—for the humans who are looking at your content. But that doesn't mean you shouldn't also optimize for search engines. You can do both.

Write two different versions of your headline. One that's designed for human readers, who appreciate style, humor, and even the occasional pun. Write a different headline that's crammed full of SEO-friendly keywords, and let Google (and your internal search engine) chew it up and spit it back out.

Taken together, that gives you four possible options:

1. Short, colloquial
2. Long, colloquial
3. Short, SEO-optimized
4. Long, SEO-optimized

You might not even need all four of these options, based on the constraints imposed by the channels you serve and your design templates. You might even work out a different system along different variables that works better for your needs. The point here is to write headlines that conform to general guidelines for length, tone, and style, and then send the right versions to the right platforms—don't create a dozen headlines to serve every possible context.

Super combo

Want extra flexibility in your headlines? Consider writing a super-header that can be displayed separately from your headline (say, called out in a different font or type size) or attached to your headline with a colon. Now you've got a short headline, a long headline, and perhaps even some category metadata. *The New York Times* employs this approach to great effect, giving them flexibility to show headlines in lots of places and contexts, achieving maximum variety with minimum effort (**FIG 6.5**).

SUMMARIES

Call it a summary, a deck, a teaser, or a tout, you need a short description for every long page of content. Not sure where you're going to use this summary? Once you've got it, you'll find all kinds of uses for it. It will come in handy for navigation teasers, as previously discussed. You can also use it on landing pages, sidebars, search results and SEO meta-descriptions, and in social media like Facebook or Pinterest.

Here's the secret: get in the habit of writing a summary whenever you create new content. It's much easier to summarize the text at the same time you create the content than it is to treat it like a separate process—or worse, have to go back and fill in summaries later, when you realize they're necessary on a new platform like mobile.

Don't truncate body text for summaries

Were you hoping you could just recycle your body text? Have your designer decide how much space your text will receive? Have your developer assign an arbitrary character count in your CMS? Drop in an ellipsis when you run out of room?

It didn't work for headlines and it didn't work for navigation teasers. It's not going to work here either.

Blockbuster has no systemic way to handle summaries for its desktop or mobile applications. Instead, they just cut the text off at an arbitrary break—and that cutoff point varies

In Afghanistan Photos, G.I.'s Posed With Body Parts

By GRAHAM BOWLEY and ALISSA J. RUBIN 1:59 PM ET

Photographs apparently showing United States soldiers with the body parts of dead insurgents drew strong condemnation on Wednesday from Defense Secretary Leon E. Panetta.

3 in Scandal Being Forced Out of Secret Service, Officials Say

By MICHAEL S. SCHMIDT
9 minutes ago

One Secret Service employee is being fired, one will retire and one will resign, according to officials and a person briefed on the matter.

Escort Recounts

Associated Press

‹ 1 2 3 4 5 ►

Dick Clark surrounded by fans on "American Bandstand" in 1957.

DICK CLARK, 1929-2012

'Bandstand' Host and New Year's Eve Icon

By BRUCE WEBER 5:10 PM ET

Mr. Clark's long-running daytime song-and-dance fest, "American Bandstand," advanced the influence of teenagers and rock 'n' roll on American culture.

· Dick Clark's Insight — Tape New Year's Stars in August
  6:27 PM ET
· Media Decoder: Reactions and Video | 🏳 Post a Comment | Read

---

U.S. »

· **Where Clean Energy Abounds, a Push to Ship Coal**

· Arizona's Illegal Immigrants Adapt to Life Under a Crackdown

· Arizona Republicans Pick Jesse Kelly for Congressional Race

Technology »

· **DealBook: With Instagram Deal, Facebook Shows Its Worth**

· DealBook: Square Said to Seek $250 Million Investment

· EBay Earnings Surpass Forecasts

Arts »

· **Dick Clark, 1929-2012: TV Host and Icon of New Year's Eve Dies at 82**

· Arts & Leisure: Filmmaker's Newest Work Is About ... Something

· Architecture Review: Quiet Additions to a Modernist Masterpiece

---

N.Y. / Region »

· **At a Brooklyn School, the Cool Crowd Pushes the King Around**

· Buses With 3 Doors? What's a Rider to Do?

· Colleagues Trace the Void Left by a Firefighter

Obituaries »

· **Dick Clark, 1929-2012: TV Host and Icon of New Year's Eve Dies at 82**

· Paul Bogart, TV Director, Dies at 92

· William Finley, Actor in De Palma Movies, Dies at 71

Theater »

· **ArtsBeat: Theater Talkback: A Good Play Can Be Read as Well as Seen**

· Theater Review: No Disney Ending for This Woodworker

· Turkish Artist Brings Audience Into the Process of Performance

---

- Dick Clark, TV Host and Icon of New Year's Eve, Is Dead at 82
- Florida Judge in Martin Case Steps Aside
- Arizona Illegal Immigrants Adapt to a Crackdown
- Boardman, Ore., Considers a Future in Coal

OPINION »

- Maureen Dowd: Phony Mommy Wars
- Thomas L. Friedman: One for the Country
- Editorial: The Big Spill, Two Years Later
- Ann Patchett: And the Winner of the Pulitzer Isn't

FIG 6.5: *The New York Times* writes surprisingly few headlines, but they can be combined in different ways and presented in various contexts.

from platform to platform. It's frustrating for the user not to be able to see the full summary—or to click for more information, only to be rewarded with a paltry few additional words (**FIG 6.6**).

Blockbuster recently filed for bankruptcy, largely due to competition from internet upstart Netflix. Netflix runs on over 400 different device types (http://bkaprt.com/csm/65). They offer different experiences tailored for each platform—but only two different sizes of summaries. Each platform can choose which size of summary to display, and it doesn't get truncated (**FIG 6.7**).

Do write a system of summaries and teasers

The magic happens when you create a single "content package" to hold *all* the chunks associated with a particular content type.

For example, don't create an article and then treat its deck like a chunk of text that only "lives" on the homepage—you'll lose the opportunity to reuse that deck in other contexts.

FIG 6.6: Blockbuster truncates text at random. The length of summaries is dictated by the design (or by an arbitrary character count) rather than by a meaningfully defined chunk of content.

FIG 6.7: Netflix writes a short and long version of each summary, each of which appears in a variety of contexts—desktop, mobile website, mobile apps, tablet apps, and search.

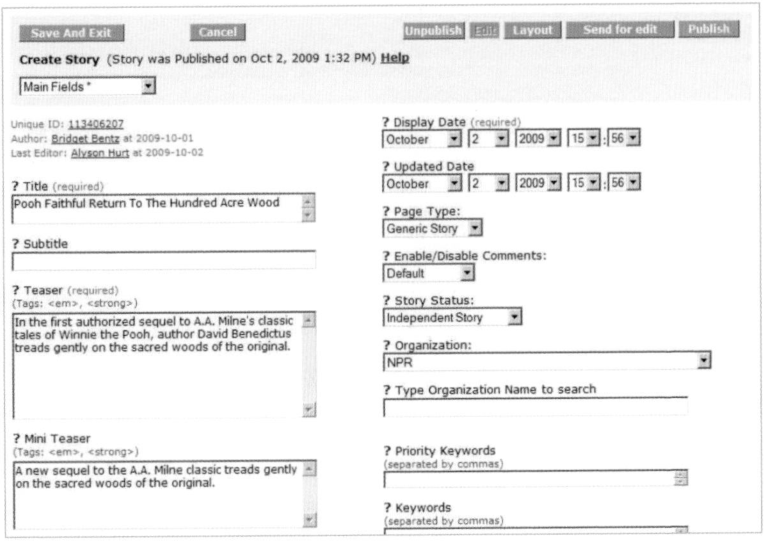

Screenshot of a CMS "Create Story" editing interface showing the following fields:

Save And Exit | Cancel | Unpublish | Edit | Layout | Send for edit | Publish

Create Story (Story was Published on Oct 2, 2009 1:32 PM) **Help**

Main Fields *

Unique ID: 113406207
Author: Bridget Bentz at 2009-10-01
Last Editor: Alyson Hurt at 2009-10-02

? Title (required)
Pooh Faithful Return To The Hundred Acre Wood

? Subtitle

? Teaser (required)
(Tags: <em>, <strong>)
In the first authorized sequel to A.A. Milne's classic tales of Winnie the Pooh, author David Benedictus treads gently on the sacred woods of the original.

? Mini Teaser
(Tags: <em>, <strong>)
A new sequel to the A.A. Milne classic treads gently on the sacred woods of the original.

? Display Date (required)
October 2 2009 15 : 56

? Updated Date
October 2 2009 15 : 56

? Page Type:
Generic Story

? Enable/Disable Comments:
Default

? Story Status:
Independent Story

? Organization:
NPR

? Type Organization Name to search

? Priority Keywords
(separated by commas)

? Keywords
(separated by commas)

FIG 6.8: NPR writes two teasers—a standard size and a mini teaser—which means each platform can choose which one to display.

Don't write a product description without also writing a summary (or two)—and ensure that the product "tout" that advertises it on landing pages is attached to the product itself. If you need to write a "meta summary" for SEO purposes, treat that as part of the same system.

See how this all keeps coming back to your content management infrastructure? Your CMS should encourage authors to create summaries—different versions of summaries as needed—guiding them through the process and explaining how each will be used. Your CMS then also needs to enable each platform to pull the proper summary for its purposes. Rather than creating one-off bits of content that live on different pages or in separate websites, each with their own editorial workflows, your CMS helps your content creators think about content packages (**FIG 6.8**).

BODY TEXT

Multiple headlines: check! System of summaries: check! Content package in the CMS: check!

Whoa. What about all these long pages of content?

As discussed earlier in the section on writing and editing, there's no such thing as writing for mobile. There's only good writing. You should think about how to improve the quality of all your text. Once you've done so, there's no need to change the substance or the style to make it more appropriate for mobile.

The challenge, then, is in how you structure your body text. This is where the proverbial rubber hits the road, as far as getting your content on mobile is concerned. What's the right way to take a long article, document, product spec, or instruction manual, and display it on different screen sizes? How do you chunk your content so it's easy to read, regardless of its visual presentation? When does it make sense to break up long pages, and when does it make sense to keep them together?

Don't paginate unnecessarily

Truncating headlines is bad. Truncating navigation teasers is bad. Truncating content summaries is bad. Truncating body copy is...

Yes. Bad.

One of mobile's most persistent myths is that content has to be short. Mobile users only want the fun-size candy bar version, preferring to save the full-size Snickers for when they're back at their desk. This misguided mindset gets drilled into designers, and as a result they fear the long page. How to avoid having mobile users wade through long passages of text? Why, break it up into shorter screens!

It's as true on mobile as it is on the desktop: scrolling is not bad. Scrolling is good!

On a touchscreen device, scrolling is much easier than paginating: a fluid swish of the thumb versus a carefully placed tap. Even if your user has to navigate with a four-way rocker, it's still easier to scroll than to select the link for "next page." If you're aiming at a user who's reading with one eye and navigating with one thumb, scrolling wins every time. So why force users to tap instead of scroll?

Advertising-supported desktop websites often include page breaks because additional page views drive revenue. If ad revenue is a motivation on mobile, then you may need to use a similar calculus to determine where page breaks should appear. *How Stuff Works* drops a page break in the middle of an article on their mobile website, even though the same article on the desktop can be read all on one page (**FIG 6.9**).

For other types of mobile content, it doesn't necessarily make sense to force a page break. If you do choose to break up text, do it for a good reason. *Cooks Illustrated* requires users to tap back and forth between the ingredients listing and the recipe instructions, even though it would be much simpler to have all that information on one page (**FIG 6.10**).

Do make it easy to jump to a section

The joy of whizzing through a page of text with a quick thumb swipe quickly wears thin when you're scanning for a specific piece of information you know is buried in the text. In the same way that it's important to provide a good teaser when the user is navigating to find a page, it's also important on mobile to make it easy to jump to a specific section of a page without scrolling.

Anchor links

Ancient hypertexts point to a good solution, one that would have worked just as well in 1995: anchor links. By pulling out headings and listing them at the top of the page, users can easily jump directly to a section without scrolling. Anchor links also serve as signposts for the main sections of a page, helping users figure out if they're in the right place (**FIG 6.11**).

FIG 6.9: *How Stuff Works* chillingly drops a page break right in the middle of a sentence. The suspense is killing me!

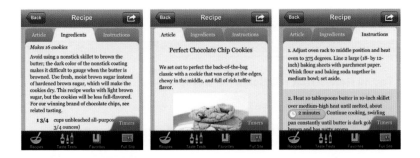

FIG 6.10: *Cooks Illustrated* forces users to jump back and forth between the ingredients and the recipe by tapping with sticky, greasy fingers. One long scrolling page would be easier to navigate.

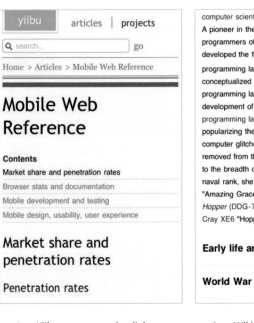

FIG 6.11: Yiibu.com uses anchor links so users can easily jump to a specific section without scrolling.

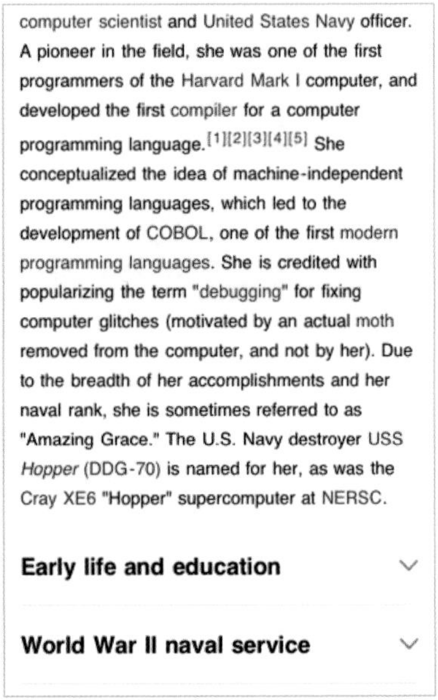

FIG 6.12: Wikipedia displays the full introduction to the article and the headers to each subsection. Users tap the heading to view the content within that section.

Show / hide

A similar solution puts each sub-section of content behind a control that can be expanded. This is particularly useful in situations where users are not likely to read the whole document, but will instead pick and choose which sections to read. However, if there's a chance users might like to read the whole thing, it would also be helpful to let them expand (and collapse) the entire page at once, so they don't have to manually tap into every section (**FIG 6.12**).

TABLES

Information arranged in tables presents one of the most vexing problems for presenting content on mobile devices. Tabular information is, by definition, intended to be presented at wider screen resolutions than many mobile devices will support. Without being able to count on a certain screen size, how is it possible to ensure that table information won't get cut off?

Don't lose table formatting

It's revenge of the blobs: content formatted for reading in table cells that gets reflowed as a single column on mobile devices. Sure, the content is still accessible, but the desired reading experience is lost. For example, side-by-side statistics on two College Bowl teams on ESPN get rendered as one long page—losing the opportunity to compare them (**FIG 6.13**).

This can be a difficult problem, especially if all that content is stored in a blob in the CMS, as finding these cases may elude all but the most manual, labor-intensive solutions. When you're inventorying your content, look carefully for tables that may break when moved to mobile. Enlist the robots to help you do this—for example, use an automated tool to find places where table tags appear in the page body.

Dealing with this problem will undoubtedly require some changes in your CMS. Based on your inventory, you should

NEW ORLEANS -- The Allstate BCS National Championship Game is finally upon us. The rematch between No. 1 LSU and No. 2 Alabama will finally be decided. Who will win? ESPN.com's Ivan Maisel and Gene Wojciechowski state their cases:

15 Reasons ...

No. 1 LSU will win *By Ivan Maisel*	No. 2 Alabama will win *By Gene Wojciechowski*

15. Home sweet Dome

You can try to measure Alabama's presence in the Superdome all you want. No matter how you calibrate it, however, LSU will still have a home-field advantage. New Orleans may be a city unto itself, but it is still a part of Louisiana. With all that is at stake, the BCS Championship Game is supposed to be played at a neutral site. This one, as were the past two at the Superdome, will not be. LSU held a distinct advantage against Oklahoma eight years ago and against Ohio State four years ago. The Tigers will have an advantage Monday night. And while you're at it, go ahead and pencil in LSU to finish in the top two in the 2015 season. If the BCS remains in its current format, that's the next time the title game will be held in New Orleans.

Superdome

15. The law of averages

I can't even pretend the Crimson Tide have better special teams than LSU. It would be like saying there aren't empty Southern Comfort bottles after a game at Tiger Stadium. It simply isn't true. Cade Foster has made exactly two more field goals in 2011 than Bear Bryant has, and Jeremy Shelley usually isn't used unless it's a sub-39-yard attempt (season-best kick: 37 yards). And who can forget what happened in the 9-6 overtime Nov. 5 loss to LSU? Nick Saban can't. Foster missed from 44, 50 and 52 yards (he's 2-of-9 for the season), and Shelley had a 49-yarder blocked. Chances are Foster and Shelley won't have to go all Janikowski again and whale away on mid-40-to-plus-50-yard attempts. And while they won't make anybody forget Leigh Tiffin, I don't see them going 2-of-6 again. If they do, they might want to consider a position change. Or a school change.

Foster

No. 1 LSU will win

By Ivan Maisel

15. Home sweet Dome

You can try to measure Alabama's presence in the Superdome all you want. No matter how you calibrate it, however, LSU will still have a home-field advantage. New Orleans may be a city unto itself, but it is still a part of Louisiana. With all that is at stake, the BCS Championship Game is supposed to be played at a neutral site. This one, as were the past two at the Superdome, will not be. LSU held a distinct advantage against Oklahoma eight years ago and against Ohio State four years ago. The Tigers will have an advantage Monday night. And while you're at it, go ahead and pencil in LSU to finish in the top two in the 2015 season. If the BCS remains in its current format, that's the next time the title game will be held in New Orleans. 15. The law of averages

14. Run, Tigers, run

In the 85-scholarship age, when coaches find developing depth is as difficult as nuclear physics, LSU uses four tailbacks to wear down defenses. Sophomores Michael Ford, Spencer Ware and Alfred Blue combined with freshman Kenny Hilliard to rush for 2,314 yards and 30

No. 2 Alabama will win

By Gene Wojciechowski

15. The law of averages

I can't even pretend the Crimson Tide have better special teams than LSU. It would be like saying there aren't empty Southern Comfort bottles after a game at Tiger Stadium. It simply isn't true. Cade Foster has made exactly two more field goals in 2011 than Bear Bryant has, and Jeremy Shelley usually isn't used unless it's a sub-39-yard attempt (season-best kick: 37 yards). And who can forget what happened in the 9-6 overtime Nov. 5 loss to LSU? Nick Saban can't. Foster missed from 44, 50 and 52 yards (he's 2-of-9 for the season), and Shelley had a 49-yarder blocked. Chances are Foster and Shelley won't have to go all Janikowski again and whale away on mid-40-to-plus-50-yard attempts. And while they won't make anybody forget Leigh Tiffin, I don't see them going 2-of-6 again. If they do, they might want to consider a position change. Or a school change.

14. Bama should have won the first time

Remember Saban's postgame presser after the LSU loss? I don't want to say he was upbeat, but it's not like you could have cooked a panini on his forehead. Instead, he seemed, well, satisfied with the Bama effort. Saban

FIG 6.13: Content from ESPN that's intended to be read side-by-side gets dumped into a single column on mobile. A better solution might be a slideshow presentation that compares two at a time.

determine if the number of tables is small enough that you can handle them as one-offs. If you have lots of tables, then you will probably need a new content type in the CMS to handle these situations. If you're dealing with many tables, you'll need a way to programmatically reformat them without human intervention—but that requires you to call them out as a separate content object from the start.

And be patient with yourself: it may not be possible to review every single page of content with a table in it before it goes live on your mobile site. Consider offering mobile users a way to flag content that's not working—an alert that says "I can't read this table" gives the user a sense of control over a broken situation, and gives you useful pointers to what needs to be fixed. You've turned an ugly error into a win-win for both you and the user.

Do ensure tables are readable

It goes without saying, right? You can't just smush a table designed for a much larger screen into a smaller space. Table columns will collapse to a point where they're too small to contain the content within, or the text will shrink until it's a meaningless blur (**FIG 6.14**).

While horizontal formatting fits easily on a desktop screen, narrower mobile screens simply can't display the full table width. Provide an alternate version where you present information in a vertical list, or align the table vertically rather than horizontally. Again, this may require defining tables as a separate content type in your CMS.

Do use progressive enhancement

Even if you're not developing a mobile website using responsive design, you can borrow progressive enhancement techniques to make your tables adapt to different screen sizes. If it's possible to choose which columns are most important, and which are less essential, then you can take a page from the progressive enhancement playbook and display only the critical columns on smaller screens. Users can tap to select

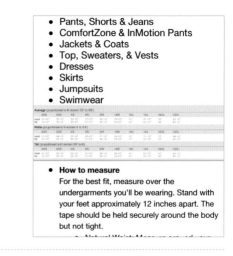

FIG 6.14: Shrink-to-fit might work for jeans, but it doesn't work for the garment size charts on New York and Company's mobile website (http://bkaprt.com/csm/66).

additional columns if they want to see the full table. (This approach would work well for a table of financial information, but wouldn't work for the garment size charts example, since in that case every column is equally important.)

The details of how to code this in markup are well beyond the scope of this book, but more information is available in the resources section in the back of the book.

IMAGES AND INFOGRAPHICS

Did I say *tables* were one of the most vexing problems we face in presenting desktop content on mobile? Tables are a cakewalk compared to the truly formidable problem that images pose.

The solution to this problem is complex, because it requires changes on both the front-end and the back-end. We'll need to crop different image sizes, which obviously means changes to our production workflow, and likely requires changes to existing assets. What's more, fixing this problem means we'll need to change the way we handle images in HTML.

How's this going to work?

Don't shrink large images

"I'm just gonna take this giant image and crunch it down so it fits on a 320×240 screen, okay?" No, this is not okay. First, the image will likely be unrecognizable when rendered at a smaller size. Details that are crisp and clear in a large image may be a blur at a smaller resolution. And if it's an infographic that includes text? Forget about it (**FIG 6.15**). Second, the larger image requires more bandwidth to download over a cell connection. A heavy image that provides less value? Not a good content strategy.

Instead, you'll need to prepare multiple versions of images (see below for more information about creating a system of image crops). The internet's love affair with dense infographics may need to find a new outlet—consider breaking large infographics down into smaller chunks presented as a slideshow. (Or, really, just quit it with the overly complex infographics and present the data more simply, in text.)

Now, if you're sitting on thousands or hundreds of thousands of large images, re-cropping them all would be a massive undertaking. In the short term, if you're forced to automatically resize large images on mobile, at least make sure users can tap to get to the full-size image.

In all cases, make sure that the information shown in the image is also communicated in the text, either in the body copy, in alt text, or both. That's not just good for mobile—it's good for accessibility and SEO too.

Don't truncate large images

"I'm just going to chop off the part of the image that won't fit on a mobile screen, okay?" (**FIG 6.16**)
Let's not even dignify this one with a response.

Do create a system of image crops

It's likely you will need to cut additional image sizes to support different screen sizes. As with all other content types, you should not plan to cut images for a specific context.

We're using smartphones for tasks and tablets for consuming richer content and leisure experiences

Display ads get more click-throughs on smartphones than tablets, which are more likely used for deeper experiences.

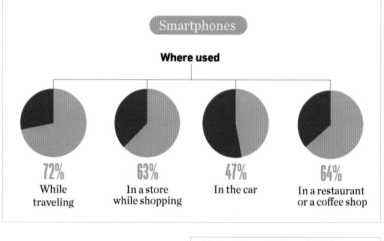

Smartphones

Where used

72%	63%	47%	64%
While traveling	In a store while shopping	In the car	In a restaurant or a coffee shop

FIG 6.15: How does *Adweek* think we use our mobiles? Apparently not to read the data that's rendered illegible in this infographic.

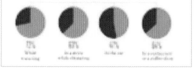

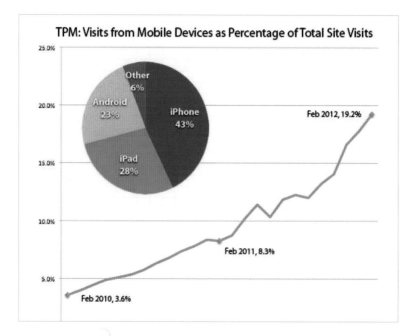

TPM: Visits from Mobile Devices as Percentage of Total Site Visits

Other 6%
Android 23%
iPhone 43%
iPad 28%

Feb 2012, 19.2%

Feb 2011, 8.3%

Feb 2010, 3.6%

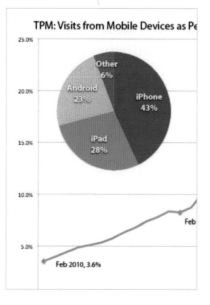

TPM: Visits from Mobile Devices as Pe

Other 6%
Android 23%
iPhone 43%
iPad 28%

Feb

Feb 2010, 3.6%

FIG 6.16: The percentage of people viewing news content on mobile phones is skyrocketing! At least, I assume that's what the truncated infographic would have shown.

Don't cut one size that's the perfect fit for your mobile website, and a slightly different size for your iPhone app. That way lies madness.

Rather, your plan should be to develop a system of image crops. Cut the smallest number of image sizes that will serve the widest possible range of contexts and screen resolutions. Assuming you can scale images down somewhat (not a lot) to fit different screens, you should be able to get away with four to eight different sizes. Exact image dimensions will be based on your specific requirements.

Keep an eye on responsive images

You don't have to go very far into responsive web design before you find very smart people banging on how to get HTML, CSS, and JavaScript to handle different image sizes. Covering the ins and outs of this lively debate is outside the scope of this book, but more information is available in the resources section.

YOU'RE ALMOST THERE

We've talked strategy and planning—you've figured out how to set a direction for where you need to go. We've discussed writing and editing, and your content should be simpler and easier to read. And we've gone over how your information architecture might change to adapt to new content structures.

Now, we need to look inside, at how your organization works. Developing a content strategy for mobile won't work if all you look at is your content. You have to change your people and your process too.

PEOPLE AND PROCESS

YOUR CONTENT isn't going to take care of itself.

Multi-channel publishing will expose the cracks and fault lines in your organization. A publishing workflow that's adequate for your desktop site (at least, most of the time) will start to crack and crumble when you begin publishing adaptive content to other channels.

You know what? That's terrific. As with so many other aspects of content strategy outlined in this book, mobile can be a catalyst to make your entire publishing process more efficient and more effective. By forcing you to focus on *how* you're going to get your content on mobile, you can make sure that all your content has clear ownership, is reviewed regularly, and is doing what it's supposed to for your readers and your business.

If you want to deliver great content, on whichever device or platform your customer wants to consume it, then you're going to need to clean house within your organization first. Here's what needs to change:

- **People:** defining leadership principles and clarifying people's roles and responsibilities has way more influence on your content's success than the technology you use for your CMS, or whether you deliver it via a mobile website or native app. Content touches every corner of your organization—mobile can force you to define who does what.
- **Process:** you'll need new metrics and measurement processes to evaluate whether your content is doing its job. Your review and approval processes will also need to change now that you're publishing your content to different platforms and devices. Don't wait until you're ready to launch a new mobile website or iPad app to define how those processes will work.

PEOPLE

Publishing to mobile means new tasks. New decisions to be accountable for. New problems to worry about.

Defining who does what, when, and why is the most important thing you can do to ensure your content delivers on every platform.

Leadership

Remember the bad old days of the web, when everyone's homepage and main navigation bar reflected the turf battles going on within the company? Your website structure shouldn't map to your org chart—it should map to how users think about their tasks and goals.

That goes double for mobile. Your users don't think they'll get different content or functionality from you just because they're using a mobile device. So don't build that distinction into your org chart.

All change requires leadership from people who are aligned on the what, why, and how. Your leaders should be able to:

- Evangelize and promote why mobile is important to executives and business owners.

- Conduct research and analyze data about how your customers use mobile—today, and in the future.
- Assemble cross-functional teams to tackle problems in mobile content delivery.
- Assign budget for investing in new mobile initiatives.
- Break through inter-departmental conflicts in terms of who "gets credit" for mobile success or failure.

Organizational structure

While the org chart is not destiny, setting up silos within your company is a risk. When planning for how to staff and deliver your mobile initiatives, you should guard against giving people incentives to think of mobile as a totally separate experience.

Your customer doesn't expect your company to be different just because they visit you on a device with a smaller screen. They know you're supposed to be all one company. So don't build conflict between mobile and your other digital channels into your org chart. Instead, figure out how to encourage your teams to create a great experience for your customer—regardless of channel, platform, or device.

Make sure there are clear lines of responsibility and reporting relationships between the mobile team and the people responsible for the desktop web. Give your team incentives to think holistically about the experience.

Don't tell your team to get a mobile site or app up quickly, without a plan for how to manage and maintain its content over time. If you do that, you run the risk of forking your content and creating an experience that's distinct from the desktop, with no plan for how you're going to keep it going.

Roles and responsibilities

Who is responsible for content in your organization? Truth be told, it's lots of different people. Representatives from "the business," IT, user experience, brand and marketing, legal, HR, PR, and communications all contribute to content on the web.

Does adding in mobile mean a whole new set of people, roles, permissions, and responsibilities? Hopefully not. Instead, your goal should be to educate and empower everyone in your organization who's currently contributing content to understand and deliver great content for mobile.

If your organization is like most others, "everyone in your organization who's currently contributing content" might be many people—even more than you expect. As with so many other examples in this book, mobile forces you to track these people down and have those conversations. If you have product owners who describe the features and benefits of their product, marketers who ask for landing pages to support their latest campaign, or social media managers who promote your company on Facebook or Twitter, then you need to align all these content creators around what you're doing on mobile. After all—if everyone is working together, everyone's job is easier.

Defining roles and responsibilities around mobile may require you to look at some or all of the following:

Content package creation

If you're planning to develop new content structures so you have more flexibility in mobile, someone needs to create them. What works for many companies is to have business content owners contribute product or marketing content as they always have—often, this is an offline process managed via Word documents, PDFs, and email. Then a dedicated editor or content strategist goes in to write new headlines, summaries, and navigation text. Mobile makes it even more critical to have an editor with a birds-eye view go over all the content systematically. In some organizations, a separate content producer is responsible for entering the content into the CMS.

Taxonomy and metadata

You need someone in your organization to maintain and review the taxonomy, tags, and other metadata used to power the site. Any changes you make can have a ripple effect across platforms, and so someone needs to understand the entire puzzle. Many organizations find that having one person to oversee the entire taxonomy and metadata means that content becomes easier to search and browse.

Media production

If you will need additional crop sizes for photos and graphics, that may be a large undertaking. Your organization will most likely need to define a project to do that, and task your creative services team (or freelancers) with getting it done.

Same goes for other media types, like Flash data visualizations or videos—someone within your team must develop fallbacks for different media types. That person or persons' role should also include making sure all your content creators know which formats they should avoid since they'll require duplicate effort for mobile.

Mobile editor

If you have a separate mobile website, or you get to the point where you want to feature or prioritize different content on mobile, consider creating a mobile editor role within your organization who programs mobile content. Keep in mind this person will also need to have different permissions with your CMS.

Having this role defined is especially important if you ever publish emergency content, or you have content that must be updated for legal reasons. In a crisis situation, the last thing you need is to have someone forget to update the mobile site.

PROCESS

The ongoing care and feeding of your content may get more complicated, as you've got more moving pieces. Let's take a look at some content aspects that you'll need to monitor as part of a regular oversight process.

Analytics

You can't do mobile content strategy correctly until you define how you're going to measure and optimize performance. Marko Hurst of Content Analytics told me this requires two things. First, you need to choose the right metrics and key performance indicators (KPIs) to measure. Second, you need the right process for getting this data—and using it to make decisions.

Measurement

You know you want to use data to inform your decisions about what to do on mobile. But which data? At the basic level, you need to track observable changes in how people are using your content on mobile. But there are lots of changes you can track, and not everything you can measure is actually useful.

Figure out what you can measure that actually reflects a change in your users' behavior—a change in behavior that would tell you to do something different within your business. At this point in your mobile content strategy, you're probably looking for changes in the way people interact with your content on both the desktop and mobile devices:

- Do you see an increase in the number of users accessing your site through mobile devices? Have you seen a corresponding decrease in visits from the desktop? This can help you determine if your customers are using mobile and the desktop interchangeably, or if you're reaching mobile-mostly users.
- Examine how your device and platform usage may vary by time of day, level of engagement, time on site, and other usage metrics. Some businesses believe that they should prioritize content differently on different platforms, or at different times of day—this data can help inform those decisions.

- Similarly, look at what type of content people are searching or browsing for from different devices. Don't rush to judgement here—make sure you have a large enough base of content and users on different devices before you make conclusions about what people want and how it varies by platform.
- Review search queries (both internal searches and external referrers) that come from mobile browsers. Focus particularly on search queries on mobile that get redirected to the mobile homepage, if you haven't optimized that content for mobile.
- If you offer a "full desktop website" link, look at exit pages where mobile users abandon your mobile site for the desktop site.

These examples are only general guidelines for what you might want to track. You need to figure out which measurements are unique to your business. Jared Spool says, "Generic KPIs produce generic results. If we really want something that touches the core of what makes our business special, it should be a metric that only applies to what we're doing," (http://bkaprt.com/csm/67).

Decision-making process

Marko Hurst told me that having the right process to evaluate the data and use it to make decisions within your organization is crucial to success. There's no point in gathering data if it doesn't help you actually do something different on mobile.

The right metrics are essential, but are only a part of the solution. You need a proven, repeatable, and rigorous process for collecting, analyzing, and acting on the data, which will allow for constant success, not random chance. Even with the right metrics, if you don't follow and refine your process for success, your "right metrics" won't matter and your level of success will be limited to little more than luck.

Too often, data like page views or unique visitors doesn't tell you anything that you can act on—this is true on the desktop web, and it's true for mobile too. Even "engagement metrics" like time on page or page bounces don't necessarily tell you anything, unless you've figured out what changes in this measurement mean to your business, and how you'll act on it when it does change.

Finally, don't think your analytics data will answer all of your questions about what people want and expect from mobile. Make sure your content governance includes a plan for user research too.

SEO

About thirty percent of global search queries come from mobile devices, and analysts estimate that by 2016, a majority of searches will be mobile searches (http://bkaprt.com/csm/68). Your content strategy for mobile needs to include search engine optimization.

But how? Standards and practices for publishing content to the mobile web are still relatively young, and SEO for mobile is still in its infancy. How should your content governance and SEO practices change?

Not at all

One compelling strategy is not to change your strategy at all. (Hooray for laziness!) Like with other recommendations in this book, it's not wise to jump into doing anything different for mobile until you understand the parameters better. Instead of trying to develop a different approach for mobile search, it's totally okay to treat desktop and mobile the same.

In fact, this seems to be the approach that Google prefers. They've indicated their preference for using responsive web design to serve the same content to all users (http://bkaprt. com/csm/69). A content strategy for mobile that doesn't distinguish between desktop content, mobile content, and tablet content—it's all just your content—may be the best SEO strategy, too.

Mobile ≠ local

If you're bugging out in disbelief that you shouldn't optimize mobile searches differently, remember one key point: just because a search is from mobile doesn't mean it's a local search. Local searches may disproportionately come from mobile devices, but one doesn't necessarily imply the other. You may need to focus on optimizing your search queries for searches that include location information, but that approach would still benefit both mobile and desktop users.

Keyword research

As part of your ongoing maintenance and governance processes, you can start evaluating whether mobile search queries use different keywords from other searches. For example:

- Are mobile searches shorter than desktop searches?
- Do mobile searches have more typos and errors than desktop searches?
- Are mobile users searching for different keywords or using different search terms?

Mobile users may use language differently. Understanding how their keyword and search term use changes might tell you that you need to assign different SEO keywords, or even modify the labels and ordering within your navigation system. As with everything else, those decisions are best made with actual data.

Approval processes

Approval processes are the "hard review" steps—the approvals built into the system that must take place before content can go live. The approval workflow needs to balance security with usability. As Jeff Eaton told me, "Everyone wants one-click publish, no one wants one-click embarrassment."

Legal review

Adaptive content creates all kinds of new challenges for legal review. Is your legal team looking at a PDF screenshot of the desktop page (or worse, a print-out) as part of their review and commenting system? What happens when they need to consider different content objects appearing in different channels?

Jeff Gladchun, J.D., Director, Digital Design Review at Fidelity Investments, told me in an email that legal review needs to move away from looking at the final presentation and into the CMS:

> *For many financial services firms, adaptive content poses unique and novel issues with respect to legal review standards and processes. In the broker-dealer context, regulations generally assume that electronic advertising can be reduced to singular communication and packaged neatly as a blob—typically a web or mobile screenshot (in PDF format, please)—for review, approval, and record keeping. Legal review systems are structured around this framework.*
>
> *Adaptive content challenges the status quo, enabling the blob to fragment into chunks which can be consumed not only by your computer or mobile device, but by your car, your refrigerator, your whatever. How do I take a screenshot of your refrigerator? I can't. So in the future, the legal review process will need to move upstream to the CMS, where the chunks can be captured in their captive state in the form of metadata before they are unleashed for public consumption.*

Business preview and QA

Many content creation processes rely on the preview function in the CMS to show the work in context. It won't be enough to rely on previewing the desktop site in the future, so put a plan in place now for how your team can preview and perform a QA review on your content in different form factors.

Will it be possible to review every possible device, screen size, and platform out there? No way. But you can identify a few of the most popular ones. Your tech team may be able to help manage this process—keep in mind that it's going to add some extra steps beyond just clicking that preview button.

CONCLUSION: IT CAN BE DONE

Are you looking dubiously at your desktop web content (not to mention all your content stored in PDFs, Flash videos, and hieroglyphic scrolls) and wondering if it will *ever* be possible to get it all on mobile?

You can. And you will. Because one day you'll realize it's not a nice-to-have. It's a necessity.

Cancer.org did it

The American Cancer Society (ACS) publishes cancer.org, a website aimed at helping people prevent cancer, detect cancer early, get support and treatment, and contribute to the fight against cancer.

If ACS were like most organizations, they might have thought the following:

"Not that many people are visiting cancer.org from their mobile browser." Or, "Surely the desktop website works well enough for mobile users." And maybe, "Let's just focus on the mobile use case, for the on-the-go cancer patient."

ACS thought something different. David Balcom, Managing Director, Digital Platforms told me in an interview, "We felt it was a life-saving imperative to have *all* of our content on mobile."

ACS decided against publishing a subset of their mobile content for a couple of reasons. First, they reviewed their analytics data and realized that people were using the desktop site from mobile browsers. This made them wonder if they needed to deliver *all* their content on mobile, instead of just a subset.

Then, they compared data about Americans who were more likely to use mobile devices to access the internet with data about people who are less likely to be screened for cancer. African Americans, Hispanics, and low-income Americans are less likely to have access to early cancer detection—and they're also more likely to use mobile phones to access the web (http://bkaprt.com/csm/70). ACS concluded that some of the most important people they needed to reach might not be able to see their content unless it was optimized for mobile.

ACS realized they needed to act. They worked quickly to get their mobile website up, working along with development partner Moovweb. But ACS had to overcome some challenges to get their content on mobile. According to Balcom, "Your CMS, your content, and your UX all have to line up."

Like many organizations, they weren't blessed with a nimble CMS that would easily facilitate everything they wanted to do on mobile. They explored the possibility of building additional publishing workflows into their CMS to give them more editorial control over which content was published to mobile, but concluded it would slow them down too much. Balcom said, "If we had created a separate workflow, it would have added a year to the process." Instead, they chose to have a single publishing workflow, with decisions about which content to show or hide happening at the server level, which reduced their time to market significantly.

Similarly, they faced technical challenges that precluded implementing a responsive design, focusing instead on creating separate templates for mobile. Balcom says they found that "responsive would have added significant time to the project," and they felt they were better off focusing on providing a great experience for smartphone users. While that decision was right for ACS, other organizations might find that a responsive design solution would be faster—it just goes to show that there's no one-size-fits-all strategy when it comes to mobile publishing.

ACS had at least one important thing in their favor: they're known for having clear, concise, credible content. Because their desktop web content was already well written, they were able to easily translate it to the mobile screen without rewriting or restructuring it. Balcom says, "It's not that it was designed and written for mobile, it's just good content." Other organizations can take this to heart: even if you're just getting started on your mobile strategy, improving your content now will benefit you in the long run.

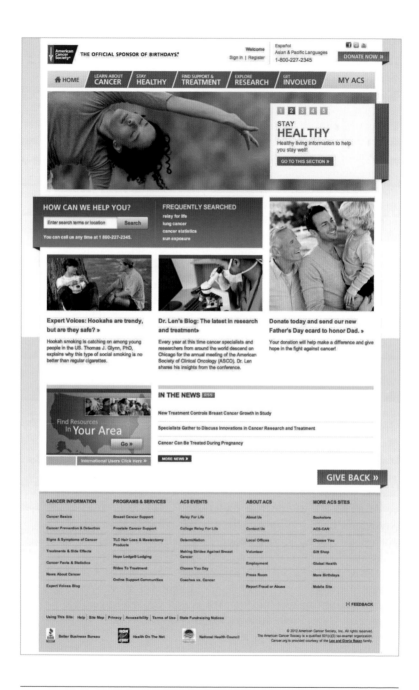

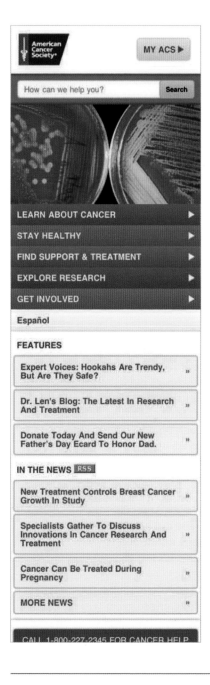

FIG 8.1: Cancer.org shows all their desktop content in a mobile-optimized website too.

Because they've been able to deliver a satisfying mobile experience, ACS has nearly doubled the number of people visiting the site from a mobile device. The increase in visits from mobile browsers shows that there was pent-up demand for better mobile content. By optimizing their content for mobile, they're getting valuable—even life-saving—information into the hands of the people who need it (**FIG 8.1**).

The secret to delivering a great experience on mobile is something every organization can do, starting right now. It's content strategy. Balcom concludes:

> *You have to get it into the bloodstream of the organization. You cannot be successful without thinking mobile from the beginning. It's not as expensive or hard as people think it is. More important: it is our future. It all starts with recognizing a gap and figuring out how to close it. It starts with a strategy.*

YOU CAN DO IT TOO

Remember: you are not in the magazine publishing business, or the brochure publishing business, or the binder publishing business. You are not in the webpage publishing business. You are not in the mobile app publishing business.

You are in the content publishing business. It is your mission to get your content out, on whichever platform, in whichever format your audience wants to consume it. Your users get to decide how, when, and where they want to read your content. It is your challenge and your responsibility to deliver a good experience to them.

To provide a great experience on mobile—one that delivers the information users want, and can be maintained internally—you need a content strategy for mobile.

Think it can't be done? Why, it's just these ten simple steps:

1. Quit thinking you can just guess what subset of content a "mobile user" wants. You're going to guess wrong.
2. Do your research, look at competitors, and evaluate your analytics data. Figure out how to convince your CEO and

your executive team (in other words, people with money) that you need a content strategy for mobile.

3. Before jumping into imagining new mobile products, figure out how you can achieve content parity across platforms. You don't have to show exactly the same content on every device, but you should provide an equivalent experience.

4. Use mobile as a catalyst to remove content that isn't providing value. Inventory and audit your content to find what's outdated, badly-written, or unnecessary. When you edit or delete it, do it to make the experience better for all your users—desktop and mobile.

5. Don't create content for a specific context or platform. It's not your desktop web content, your mobile web content, your tablet content, your email content, your social content, or even your print content. It's just your content.

6. Instead, create content packages: a flexible system of content elements that cover a range of possible places where your content might get used. Then manage and maintain those content elements all in one place.

7. Develop a process and workflow that will support and enable maximum content reuse with minimum additional effort. That's *adaptive content:* structured content that's created so that it can be reused.

8. Separate content from form and create presentation-independent content. Don't encode meaning through visual styling—you'll have to strip it out when you move to another platform. Instead, add structure and metadata to your content.

9. Ensure that your content management tools make it easy—and possible—for your content creators to develop the content structures needed to support adaptive content. This is a user experience problem for CMS design.

10. Invest in CMS frameworks that support multi-channel publishing. If you're imagining a future where you have finer control over which content you publish to mobile, desktop, and everything in-between, then you've got work to do to make sure your tools, processes, and workflow will support that.

Still think it's daunting? It is. It's also a huge opportunity—maybe the best we'll see in our careers—to change the way we create, manage, and maintain our content. And it's a big chance to create a better user experience by improving the quality of our content. Let's not waste it.

RESOURCES

Progressive enhancement for tables

Presenting complex, multi-column data on small screens is both a design and a content strategy challenge. These resources provide some background on the magnitude of the challenge and show prototypes that offer concrete workarounds.

- A Responsive Design Approach for Complex, Multicolumn Data Tables, Filament Group (http://bkaprt.com/csm/71)
- Responsive Tables Demo, Simon Elvery (http://bkaprt.com/csm/72)
- A New Take on Responsive Tables, ZURBlog (http://bkaprt.com/csm/73)
- Responsive Data Table Roundup, CSS-Tricks (http://bkaprt.com/csm/74)

Responsive images

Handling different sizes and formats of images is a content strategy problem, a front-end problem, a back-end problem... well, just a big problem. These resources explain why images are so difficult to handle, and offer some solutions (and potential future solutions).

- Responsive images: what's the problem, and how do we fix it?, Dev.Opera (http://bkaprt.com/csm/75)
- Responsive Images: How they Almost Worked and What We Need, Mat Marquis (http://bkaprt.com/csm/76)
- Which responsive images solution should you use?, CSS-Tricks (http://bkaprt.com/csm/77)
- Picturefill, Scott Jehl (http://bkaprt.com/csm/78)

Research and testing on mobile

Even if you're familiar with conducting user research and usability tests of desktop websites, you may find that mobile presents a whole new set of challenges. Make sure you're testing with the right people, the right methods, in the right context, and with the right devices with these resources.

- Mobile user research methods, Lorraine Paterson (http://bkaprt.com/csm/79)
- 10 Tips for Mobile Usability Testing, Trent Mankelow (http://bkaprt.com/csm/80)
- How to Build a Device Lab, Dave Olsen (http://bkaprt.com/csm/81)
- Mobile Device Testing: The Gear, Bagcheck (http://bkaprt.com/csm/82)

Mobile SEO

Like so many other topics in this space, search engine optimization for mobile is a rapidly changing landscape. And, as with so much of search engine optimization, the topic is subject to hype and fierce debates. These resources attempt to sort out what we know about what users (and search engines) want.

- Google Finally Takes A Clear Stance On Mobile SEO Practices, Barry Schwartz (http://bkaprt.com/csm/83)
- Mobile SEO is a Myth, Ryan Jones (http://bkaprt.com/csm/84)
- Mobile SEO Best Practices, MobiThinking (http://bkaprt.com/csm/85)

REFERENCES

Shortened URLs are numbered sequentially; the related long URLs are listed below for reference.

Chapter 1

1 http://blog.nielsen.com/nielsenwire/online_mobile/double-vision-global-trends-in-tablet-and-smartphone-use-while-watching-tv/

2 http://mobithinking.com/mobile-marketing-tools/latest-mobile-stats/d#mobile-search

3 http://www.ljs.com/images/docs/smart_phones_create_smart_shoppers.pdf

4 http://www.pewinternet.org/Reports/2012/In-store-mobile-commerce/Findings.aspx

5 http://www.tealeaf.com/news/news-releases/2011//Tealeaf-Announces-New-Mobile-Research.php

6 http://www.acquitygroup.com/News-And-Ideas/News/Acquity-Group-Mobile-Audit-Reports-210--Increase-i

7 http://static.googleusercontent.com/external_content/untrusted_dlcp/www.google.com/en/us/events/thinkmobile2011/pdfs/time-for-mobile-is-now.pdf

8 http://www.scribd.com/webrazzi/d/82693519-ComScore-2012-Mobile-Future-in-Focus

9 http://pewinternet.org/Commentary/2010/September/The-Power-of-Mobile.aspx

10 http://blog.nielsen.com/nielsenwire/online_mobile/survey-new-u-s-smartphone-growth-by-age-and-income/

11 http://pewinternet.org/Reports/2011/Smartphones/Section-2/Smartphones-as-an-internet-appliance.aspx

12 http://www.pewinternet.org/Reports/2012/Teens-and-smartphones/Cell-phone-ownership/Smartphones.aspx

13 https://twitter.com/wilto/statuses/63284673723375616

14 http://www.slate.com/articles/technology/technology/2011/08/overdone.single.html

15 https://twitter.com/cennydd/status/61004881011539968

16 http://blog.securecube.com/web-apps/browser-display-statistics/

17 http://mobithinking.com/mobile-marketing-tools/latest-mobile-stats/a

18 http://mobithinking.com/blog/china-top-mobile-market

19 http://mobithinking.com/mobile-research-casestudy

20 http://www.pewinternet.org/Reports/2012/Cell-Internet-Use-2012.aspx

21 http://www.pewinternet.org/Reports/2012/Digital-differences/Main-Report/The-power-of-mobile.aspx

22 http://pewinternet.org/Reports/2012/Digital-differences/Main-Report/Internet-adoption-over-time.aspx

23 http://pewinternet.org/Commentary/2012/February/Pew-Internet-Mobile.aspx

24 http://blog.nielsen.com/nielsenwire/online_mobile/two-thirds-of-new-mobile-buyers-now-opting-for-smartphones/

25 http://www.idc.com/getdoc.jsp?containerId=prUS23028711

26 http://www.guardian.co.uk/technology/2011/feb/09/ken-olsen-obituary

27 http://www.pewinternet.org/Reports/2012/Just-in-time/Main-Report/Findings.aspx

28 http://venturebeat.com/2012/07/31/facebook-mobile-maus/

29 http://www.netmagazine.com/features/10-must-see-sessions-sxsw-interactive

30 http://blogs.msdn.com/b/jensenh/archive/2006/03/31/565877.aspx

31 https://twitter.com/#!/grigs/status/200577176314191872

Chapter 2

32 http://www.useit.com/alertbox/mobile-vs-full-sites.html

33 http://www.netmagazine.com/news/designers-respond-nielsen-mobile-121892

34 http://www.netmagazine.com/opinions/nielsen-wrong-mobile

35 http://www.usa.gov/webreform/state-of-the-web.pdf

36 http://www.netmagazine.com/interviews/nielsen-responds-mobile-criticism

37 http://www.modelmetrics.com/wp-content/uploads/2011/05/iPadSurvey-May10.pdf

38 http://www.observer.com/2011/07/scott-dadich-ipad-conde-nast/

39 http://bits.blogs.nytimes.com/2011/02/04/a-race-between-digital-and-print-magazines/?pagewanted=all

40 http://paidcontent.org/2012/02/22/419-conde-nast-aims-to-unify-tablet-and-mobile-magazine-production/

Chapter 3

41 http://bradfrostweb.com/blog/web/for-a-future-friendly-web/

42 http://www.slideshare.net/danieljacobson/npr-examples-of-cope

43 http://mashable.com/2012/05/08/google-seo-headlines/

44 http://mashable.com/2011/08/29/social-media-case-studies/

45 http://www.businessweek.com/magazine/scott-forstall-the-sorcerers-apprentice-at-apple-10122011.html

46 http://gawker.com/5847344

47 http://nymag.com/news/features/nypd-2012-4/

48 http://www.thedailybeast.com/newsweek/2011/10/16/herman-cain-s-unlikely-republican-rise.html

49 http://www.nytimes.com/2012/04/15/magazine/republicans-who-supported-gay-marriage.html?pagewanted=all

50 http://nimble.razorfish.com/

51 http://techguylabs.com/

52 http://www.markboulton.co.uk/journal/comments/responsive-content-is-not-a-thing

53 http://think-info.com/2012/03/26/separating-content-from-presentation/

54 http://groups.google.com/group/contentstrategy/browse_thread/thread/5c1770a39994b55a/05964588b922a0b6?lnk=gst&q=eoin#05964588b922a0b6

55 http://adage.com/article/media/sale-tv-guide-1-a-shock-a-surprise/131849/

56 http://bunchedundies.blogspot.com/2011/11/tv-guide-september-14-1985.html

57 http://www.markporter.com/notebook/?p=1080

58 https://twitter.com/textfiles/status/119403173436850176

59 http://dswillis.com/uxcrank/?p=378

Chapter 4

60 https://developers.google.com/analytics/devguides/collection/other/mobileWebsites

61 http://insights.chitika.com/2012/study-apple-ipad-accounts-for-94-64-of-all-tablet-web-traffic/

62 http://www.comscore.com/Press_Events/Press_Releases/2012/4/Kindle_Fire_Captures_more_than_Half_of_Android_Tablet_Market

Chapter 6

63 http://www.uie.com/brainsparks/2008/09/27/journal-of-usability-studies-articles-lacking-in-usability/

64 http://www.interaction-design.org/encyclopedia/progressive_disclosure.html

65 http://www.lukew.com/ff/entry.asp?1339

66 http://wtfmobileweb.com/post/21777271474/completely-unreadable-garment-size-charts-on-new

Chapter 7

67 http://www.uie.com/articles/power_of_ux_kpi/

68 http://allthingsd.com/20120210/heres-what-apple-and-google-are-fighting-over-search-goes-mobile-by-2016/

69 http://searchengineland.com/google-finally-takes-a-clear-stance-on-mobile-seo-practices-123543

Conclusion

70 http://www.pewinternet.org/Reports/2012/Cell-Internet-Use-2012/Main-Findings/Cell-Internet-Use.aspx

Resources

71 http://filamentgroup.com/lab/responsive_design_approach_for_complex_multicolumn_data_tables/

72 http://elvery.net/demo/responsive-tables/

73 http://www.zurb.com/article/982/a-new-take-on-responsive-tables

74 http://css-tricks.com/responsive-data-table-roundup/

75 http://dev.opera.com/articles/view/responsive-images-problem/

76 http://www.alistapart.com/articles/responsive-images-how-they-almost-worked-and-what-we-need/

77 http://css-tricks.com/which-responsive-images-solution-should-you-use/

78 https://github.com/scottjehl/picturefill

79 http://lorrainepaterson.wordpress.com/2011/02/22/mobile-user-research-methods/

80 http://www.optimalusability.com/2012/01/10-tips-for-mobile-usability-testing/

81 http://www.dmolsen.com/mobile-in-higher-ed/2012/06/26/how-to-build-a-device-lab-part-1/

82 https://bagcheck.com/blog/22-mobile-device-testing-the-gear

83 http://searchengineland.com/google-finally-takes-a-clear-stance-on-mobile-seo-practices-123543

84 http://www.searchenginejournal.com/mobile-seo-is-a-myth/35012/

85 http://mobithinking.com/best-practices/mobile-seo-best-practices/

ACKNOWLEDGEMENTS

I've been blessed by the support of so many colleagues and friends over the course of my career, but never more so than during the writing of this book. No one would be holding this book in their hands right now if it weren't for these people.

To Jeffrey Zeldman, Eric Meyer, Toby Malina, Marci Eversole, and the entire team at An Event Apart, thank you for inviting me to speak at so many of your events—and for encouraging me to expand one of my talks into this book. I'm a better speaker and writer because I've held myself to the high standards you set.

To Mandy Brown, Max Fenton, Casson Rosenblatt, Jason Santa Maria, Krista Stevens, and Rob Weychert—all the wonderful people at A Book Apart who make these great books happen—thank you for making this process go so smoothly, and for making my ideas look and sound better than I ever could on my own. You make a hard job look so easy.

To Paul Ford, thank you for writing the foreword to this book. It would be an honor just to have my name alongside yours on some scrap of paper, like a receipt or a Post-It note. Seeing your name on the cover of this book is an endless source of delight.

To Travis Harwood and Diana Turner, thank you for your enthusiasm and commitment to helping to research what we thought was going to be a whitepaper or report. If it weren't for your focus and attention to this project, this book would have never happened. And to everyone I've worked with over the years at Bond Art + Science, especially Jenny Ng, Michael Dekker, and Jon Greacen, thank you for making me so much smarter about how the web works.

To David Balcom, Gerard Gober, Marko Hurst, Jeffrey Gladchun, Noz Urbina, and Rich Ziade, thank you for agreeing to be interviewed in support of my research for this book, and for being patient with my many questions. It's because of your thoughtful and innovative approach to your work that our field is evolving so quickly, and for the better.

To Jeff Eaton, Rachel Lovinger, Stephen Turbek, and Luke Wroblewski, thank you for taking the time to read a draft of this book and provide your feedback. I knew I could count on you to push me to tighten my arguments and perfect my examples. I'm not sure whether I'm more proud to consider you all esteemed colleagues or trusted friends.

To my mother Gerry, my father Mike, and my step-father John, thank you for teaching me a sense of humor and the ability to write and communicate well. It's really been the whole foundation of my success in life, and the best heirloom I could have received.

And especially to Randy Bender, Bill DeRouchey, Joe Fusco, Kristina Halvorson, Amanda Neville, Victor Preuninger, Paula Riley, Steve Schneider, Jai Sen, Alex Snell, Samantha Soma, and Carolyn Wood, thank you for your kindness, generosity, loyalty, and compassion during the parts of writing and editing this book that were the most painful for me. In small ways and large, each of you showed me what it means to be a true friend.

INDEX

ABOUT A BOOK APART

Web design is about multi-disciplinary mastery and laser focus, and that's the thinking behind our brief books for people who make websites. We cover the emerging and essential topics in web design and development with style, clarity, and, above all, brevity—because working designer-developers can't afford to waste time.

The goal of every title in our catalog is to shed clear light on a tricky subject, and do it fast, so you can get back to work. Thank you for supporting our mission to provide professionals with the tools they need to move the web forward.

COLOPHON

The text is set in FF Yoga and its companion, FF Yoga Sans, both by Xavier Dupré. Headlines and cover are set in Titling Gothic by David Berlow.

ABOUT THE AUTHOR

If the internet is more awesome than it was in 1995, Karen would like to claim a very tiny piece of the credit. For more than fifteen years Karen has helped create more usable digital products through the power of user experience design and content strategy. She founded Bond Art + Science in 2006, and has led content strategy and information architecture engagements for *The Atlantic, Fast Company,* Franklin Templeton, and Fidelity.

Previously, Karen helped build the User Experience practice at Razorfish, hired as the very first information architect and leaving as the VP and national lead for user experience. There she led major design initiatives for *The New York Times,* Condé Nast, Disney, and Citibank, and managed a diverse team of information architects, content strategists, and user researchers.

Karen teaches Design Management in the MFA in Interaction Design program at the School of Visual Arts in New York, which aims to give students the skills they need to run successful projects, teams, and businesses. She is also VP of digital for consulting and venture capital firm Ignite Venture Partners.

Karen's only professional experience is in content strategy and user experience design, work she pursued after receiving an M.S. in Technical Communication from Rensselaer Polytechnic Institute, where she focused her research on interface design and usability.

Photo by Alison Grippo